SoulThriver

The Story of One Woman's Journey
From Victim to Survivor to Thriver

By **SARAH CLAIMBRIDGE**

This book is dedicated to my husband and son who without their love and support of me and my growth this work would not have become a reality. Thank you to Jay for his faith in me and in what I have to share. Thank you to Patricia for her keen eye and honest feedback. And a big thanks you to all my anonymous friends from A-Z.

I am now a thriver living life for the highest good with my soul intact, I am a SoulThriver. I have a deep connection with the Universe. I see synchronicities in everyday life that tell me I am a part of the deep healing stream of consciousness that flows around me. I am on my path to be a SoulThriver Master, in order to help myself and others.

Preface:

Friends can hardly believe my story.
Neither can I.
I am so distant from the person I was.
I love and cherish my young self but she is light years away
from where I am now.
The stories you will read are all true.
Healing is possible.
Thriving is precious and attainable.
I did it, so can you!

PROLOGUE

In the middle of the night I was jolted awake by the blood-curdling sounds of crumpling metal, tree branches snapping and rocks tumbling into each other. *Reminds me of the shock and panic I felt when my father came to my bed during the night.* My husband Ralph and I leapt out of bed. We called 911. In our night clothes, we rushed up the hill behind our house onto the road that wound around the mountain behind us. We found nothing but quiet darkness and an eerie brown cloud of dust hanging in the air. *Much like the trauma of incest, something horrible has happened here, only the after effects are barely visible.*

The air was filled with a sense of tragedy but we saw nothing out of place. Several neighbors have also arrived but we found nothing, so all returned to their homes. Except Ralph and I. *I am left with a tragedy that I cannot comprehend.* I must find out what happened. As I looked down the short distance to my house, I noticed broken branches, damaged trees and tire marks. The hill was steep and slippery with fine dust. *I recognize the wreckage that incest has caused me, seen and unseen, which others are not aware of.* I slowly followed the tire marks, ducking under broken branches. The hill was getting steeper and I had to crouch and scoot along on my butt, holding on to branches to keep from sliding down. *It is the drop down into the shadow. It is treacherous, dirty, an uncharted path.* It was hard to see anything. Suddenly, there in the bushes, I could make out the back end of a car; it was a little red Honda Civic. *The car, in dream analysis, represents our bodily vehicle. It is red, I have red hair.*

As I struggled to get down to the car, I noticed sunshades on the windows, the kind used to protect children. My heart started to race. Was there a child in the car? Or maybe a baby? *I am searching for a wounded child, my inner wounded child.* I looked and found the back seat empty then realized that the "sunshades" I saw were deployed air bags. I crawled to the driver's side window and found a young woman in scrubs, unconscious, with her head resting on the steering wheel. *Scrubs, looking a lot like pajamas. My traumatic experience with my father happens most of the time while I am wearing my pajamas.*

The woman awoke and frantically tried to open the car door. It wouldn't budge. It had remained partially caught beneath the dirt of the hill, which had actually stopped it from careening further down and into our house. *Her fear is my fear as I desperately try to remove myself from danger, and the possibility that I will cause myself further damage.* I asked her name, and she replies, Sarah. *My name is Sarah.* Uncertain whether or not she was injured, I told her to stay in the car. *Incest rarely has visible scars causing victims and others to believe that there is no real damage or that children easily are able to forget, forever, what happened to them.*

Because our 911 call had gone to the distant Highway Patrol instead of the nearby Fire Department, no help had yet arrived. *Assistance to this life threatening abuse is very difficult to get. Rescuers cannot see behind closed doors. If help is sought, few people will willingly help a child who is hurting. This is a terribly unpleasant subject that most will avoid.* The fifteen minutes that elapsed since we dialed 911 felt like forever. *When help is offered it is usually a painful and slow process for those who are being rescued.*

I climbed back up the hill and we waved down an approaching vehicle. There are three women in the car. *These represent my three sisters.* We pleaded with them to stop at the Fire Station and tell them that we needed help, but they had been drinking and were not willing to stop. *My three sisters are unable to help when young and as adults they are numbing themselves with drugs and alcohol to numb the painful truth of our childhood. They do not seek help.* My husband stayed on the road. *My husband looks for help for me. He is always willingly helping me on my path to recovery.*

I climbed back down the hill to where Sarah was and found her on the phone. She's saying she doesn't know where she is or what has happened. *Abuse makes me feel disconnected, disoriented and far from my body.* I took the phone, it was her stepfather. I told him where we were, that Sarah seemed okay, and that help was on the way. I felt a connection with her step-father. *The Universe has brought me him, instead of her birth father. Many incest stories involve step-fathers. Several members of therapy group are appalled that I suffered the incest at the hands of my father. They have always believed that their father would never do such a thing and because of my circumstances I always think step-fathers must be better than real fathers.* He told me that Sarah worked nights at the local hospice and that she just recently purchased her car. *This would have been a perfect job for me, caretaking the helpless and being awake during the night as I suffer from night terrors.*

She was going in and out of consciousness. *The abuse causes me to float between my real and unreal reality.* I woke her up each time and tried to calm her panic. She has wrecked her brand new car. *The damage to myself is wreckage, like Sarah, I am overcome with guilt and shame.*

Her phone rang, she answered it, and I can hear a man's voice, her boyfriend, abusing her, yelling and cussing. *My first husband was terribly abusive, verbally, physically, mentally, emotionally and sexually.* I took the phone from Sarah, told him she was okay and that help was on the way. *I am taking control away from my abusive first husband.* The boyfriend continued to yell and curse so I hung up and refused to answer his numerous calls. *After several attempts I finally am able to break away from my ex-husband and have the strength to refuse his requests, demands and threats.*

I then saw red lights flash above me. It was the Fire Department, at last. The firemen asked about possible access from below and I explained to them that there was a creek, trees, rocks and steep slopes below me and that coming down the hill from the road was their best option. It took several minutes for me to convince them that I knew the terrain and the best way to reach Sarah. *On my path to recovery I come up against those who challenge my knowledge and experience.* As they were preparing to lower climbing ropes, Sarah's stepfather arrived. He said he was a tree trimmer and normally had his climbing equipment with him, but he had driven a different vehicle and so he can only observe. *Though her step-father wants to rescue her, much like I imagine a step-father would rescue me, he is not equipped with the proper tools or knowledge to help me heal from the incest.* Sarah's mother was not with him. *My own mother is not there for me. She has sacrificed me to my father.*

The firemen lowered the ropes, climbed down and prepared Sarah to be carried out. *My help finally arrives in the form of therapists, books, therapy groups and 12-step meetings.* Once she was safely out, the last fireman attached a harness to me and to himself. We began to be pulled up. *I am cradled in his lap. I am in the assisted birthing position with the fireman supporting my body. I am rebirthing myself.* It was difficult as we slipped from side to side. *My rebirthing process is difficult, arduous and slippery.* On the way up, I lost one of my raggedy old red house slippers. I was ashamed of how they look to strangers but, because I love them so much, I must have the lost one retrieved. He agreed to get it for me. *I learn to take ownership of who I am and that the things I treasure are worth treasuring. I own my shame and transform it into something I can happily accept. My ugly slipper is 'MY' ugly slipper.*

Upon reaching the road and removing the harness, I received a hug from Sarah's stepfather. *I have support on my path to recovery in my new friends.* Sarah was already on her way to the hospital. *Yes I, Sarah, am being helped.* I soon realized that the Fire Captain in charge was a man I worked with at the Fire Department's Headquarters. *This brings me back into my body and into my reality. Due to an injury I received at work I was fired. This once caused me great shame until I realized, years later, how much the Fire Department had improved by my actions and how all the employees continued to benefit from my having worked there.* We share what has happened in our lives since we last talked.

A tow truck arrived to pull Sarah's car back up the hill to the road. It was a complicated and difficult job retrieving the wrecked car and in doing so, the car is even further damaged, beyond repair. *There is sorrow and pain in my journey to recovery. It is complicated and difficult. It feels as though I am being re-abused as I re-live the abuse. The truth is very painful. Unlike Sarah's car, I am not a total loss. I am repairable. I can be made better than when I was new.*

We returned home for a couple of hours sleep. The date was May 5th, my mother's birthday.

CHAPTER ONE

It was May 1959, one week after my mother had turned twenty and we were living in Southern California. She was not yet old enough to legally drink or vote. She was at the hospital giving birth to her fourth child. At home, my father took me to their bedroom where he undressed and sat on the bed. He had me sit next to him; he took my hand and made me touch him, masturbate him. The moment my hand touched his skin, I recoiled. It feels like my outer skin shattered, my sense of security evaporated as I sensed the betrayal of my innocence. My father, my protector, had now become the bad guy. I escaped into my mind. My focus drifted toward the ceiling. I didn't know it at the time, but I would never be the same.

My four-year-old self could not comprehend the enormity of what has just happened. At four years old, I knew that this felt bad, wrong, and I couldn't understand why my father did not also realize this. Nothing was communicated to me by my father, yet I understood that I was not to tell anyone what has just happened, and continued to happen. This was the beginning of a long string of events that shaped me on my path to become a SoulThriver.

I am the oldest of four girls, with fewer than five years between us. My three sisters are beautiful blonde blue-eyed California girls, and I am not. I am a freckly redhead. We were four babies being raised by very young parents with few or no parental skills. We were taught that our existence caused our parents stress and anxiety, a lesson that permeates ourselves, always.

My mother tells me that I was a happy baby until my sister Ruth was born when I was sixteen months old. She said I was so mad at her and my father that I wouldn't look at them for weeks. Less than three and a half years later, there were two moreWhen my mother was pregnant with the fourth, our father badly wanted a son. He had us convinced that the new baby was a boy. When they brought the baby girl home, we were told that 'his' name was Barney Google, with the goo-goo-googliest eyes. We knew she was a girl but called her Barney until she was old enough to declare that her name was Lynn, not Barney. Lynn was a rebel, bringing into our lives a fierceness that the rest of us girls needed in order to survive our parents.

My world had suddenly changed. I had three little sisters and my father was molesting me. My mother thought that, with all the attention my father was giving me, I must be his favorite. I had red hair like my mother. My maternal grandmother, Grandma Jane and I were redheaded, left-handed, with blue eyes. Mother was the younger of two girls. Her older sister, from another father, was named after their mother and my mother was named after her mother's sister. When my mother was four years old my faithfully Catholic grandmother dropped her, and her sister, off at a nunnery. The nuns immediately took a scrub brush to my mother's red head and tried to scrub "that devil color" out of her hair. Grandma Jane, like a good Irish, was raised in the Catholic Church and attended Catholic school. Grandma, being redheaded and left-handed, was doubly afflicted with the devil's mark. When she died at seventy-six you could still see the scars on her left hand where the nuns used rulers to beat the devil out of her.

While kept at the nunnery, my mother says she spent her time plotting their escape. They were rescued by their mother's sister, my mother's namesake. On Christmas that year, at her aunt's house, she was given a doll, the first gift she had ever received. Eventually, they were retrieved by their mother. Grandma Jane loved to party, entertaining lots of men, spilling over to her under-aged daughters, where they were sexually abused by these men.

Grandma Jane told me that when she was young she adored her father. They owned the first dairy in town. She would ride in the back of the wagon and help him deliver milk to the local businesses. She also loved riding on the back of her brother's motorcycle, until one day her mother discovered what her brother was doing to her innocent body during these outings. Grandma Jane was severely punished. She was made to sit in boiling water, and then placed in the closet. Her brother suffered no punishment.

I come from a long line of incest, sexual abuse, and abusive mothers. Unlike the women before me, as an adult, I had access to therapies, gained coping skills, and was living in a world that was beginning to change the way it looked at incest. I would pioneer a shift in our lineage towards surviving, to eventually thriving.

We grew up in a small Southern California town. My parents were part hippie and part isolationist. We grew our own food, raised chickens for eggs and rabbits for meat that we sold at the corner market. We did the house chores, yard chores and took care of the animals. Our father had told us that, when he was young, he was a girl but that he grew into a man, and that we girls would grow into men, too, so we must learn men's work. To further this 'truth,' the townspeople called us "The Miller Boys."

The small town life had a quiet, slow, and peaceful pace. Everyone knew everyone. Our differences were as basic as to what church we attended. Most men did the same type of work. We never locked our doors and during the hot summer nights, we left all the doors and windows open. The real danger for me was *inside* our house.

Saturdays my mother would do her grocery shopping at the store in the next town. While she was gone we girls stayed home and played. It was then when my father, in a strange voice, would call me into the house. He took me to their bedroom where I "disappeared." He would undress, hand me a tissue, and make me masturbate him. He would tell me when to place the tissue over the end of his penis while he ejaculated, and then he sent me out. I flushed the tissue down the toilet and then I walked outside. Like a zombie.

After a couple of minutes I would store the experience somewhere deep, deep inside and try to be a little girl once again. I knew that my sisters sensed something unspeakable was happening to me when our father called me into the house. Later, when I'd come back out to play, there was a dark cloud that always enveloped us four, but we never spoke about it. The cloud would slowly dissipate and we would then find some activity to distract us.

One of our favorite activities was to each take a baby rabbit from the nesting boxes, carrying them to the freshly mowed lawn. There we made little grass nests with the clippings, placing our bunnies inside, as they safely nibbled on the grass. We knew it was not safe for the bunnies to be held in our hands. We had talked about how much our hands wanted to squeeze them flat. I believe this was a result of the tension we held in our bodies. Luckily, we never acted on these impulses. The bunnies were unharmed and grew to be adult rabbits. As sisters, we shared a lot about what we

4

were feeling, though we never talked about the times our father called me into the house. This was the beginning of keeping secrets and storing shame within me.

After our father left for work each day, and we had eaten breakfast, mother would send us outside and lock the doors. She was locking herself in and us out. We had to use the yard for our bathroom. When my father discovered what we were doing he laughed because this was such a 'boy' thing. We were four ragamuffins who began showing up daily at the gas station next door, needing a place to pee and poop. We were so ashamed. They eventually started locking the door and we had to beg them to open it for us.

I remember meeting my maternal grandfather for the first time when I was five. He and my mother hadn't seen each other since she was small. He had a new family and had heard that she had given birth to her fourth daughter. He made us laugh and he seemed like a nice man. When it was time for me to go to kindergarten the next morning, I did not want to leave. I was sad that my sisters got to stay home with him, but he assured me that he would be there when I got home. I ran home after school to find that he had left. I never saw my grandfather again. We never spoke of him again. Growing up, my mother told me frequently how lucky I was to have a father, as she never had one in her life. I tried to accept the idea that I was lucky to have a father and if he chose to molest me that it was just his way of showing me that he loved me.

We lived in a little yellow house where the front faced a quiet street where we learned to ride bikes and the back faced the busy main street. There was a motorcycle cop that parked on the main drag up the incline of our backyard. I liked climbing up the fence to visit with him and admire his motorcycle. I fantasized that he was my protector and would help me if I ever got the nerve to tell him what my father was doing.

I was a strong-headed child. The first day of kindergarten, I tried to take charge of all the other children and unsuccessfully directed them on how to hang their jackets. I was so used to being in charge at home and having my audience of three do whatever I wished; I was flabbergasted when the kids at school didn't listen. I loved teaching my sisters new things. One morning, as I was getting ready to go to kindergarten, I gathered my sisters into the bathroom and decided to show them how to brush their teeth. My mother found the four of us poised over the toilet, toothbrushes in hand. She pointed out that I had used my father's hair cream instead of toothpaste.

When we were all ill, our mother took our temperature orally. Upon my secret command, we all bit down at once and broke the glass thermometers, spilling the mercury contents all over. This wasn't our first experience with mercury. We had found a quart jar tucked away in the back of the shelf in the chicken shed. It was a brown bottle covered in dust and filled with a magical substance inside. I was convinced that some strange creatures shared our world and had left this jar for our pleasure. We had hardwood floors in our house and this fairy-like silver substance fascinated us as we dropped handfuls onto the floor. It turned into beads and scattered everywhere. We would gather it back up again into liquid reflecting pools. We loved rubbing the silky mesmerizing liquid on our faces and arms. We never told our parents of our find and for years my father swore to his friends that mercury evaporated, as the amount in the jar decreased over time.

Growing up on a small farm was unique in our town. I enjoyed operating the tractor we used to plow and till with. It was like a large rototiller with a mind of its own. I enjoyed being the captain of this rusty red, blade-churning land boat as it was very strong and could be quite dangerous. I could barely look over the top of it. It was loud and took all of my attention to do the job right. I was excited to develop my skills for when I would become a man and I wanted my father to be proud of me. I created long furrows in which we planted corn kernels. We fertilized the corn by burying fish heads in the holes along with the kernels. Once the corn reached its full height and started to produce ears, it became my magical world of escape where I could hide and imagine I was a different girl in a different world. Snakes loved to hang out in the corn fields, hunting for gophers. We understood that the snakes were beneficial and didn't kill them, though our neighbors felt differently and frequently chopped their heads off with a shovel or hoe. In the movies you see lovers frolicking in the corn fields or people being chased by bad guys. In reality, if you are not careful, the corn leaves are like serrated knives and will give you nasty cuts. My newly created escape came with dangers and was not the safe retreat I had imagined for myself. I also discovered that playing in the hay is not like it is in the movies either. Hay is really sharp, pokes the heck out of you and it is very hard to get out of long hair.

We lived on an acre of land and made the most of it. We always had chickens that were great for eating the bugs in the garden and laying tasty eggs. When they no longer produced eggs they were butchered for our dinner. I did not like butchering time. Once I saw my father preparing to butcher a rooster that was suffering from some kind of disease and was in pain. My father tried to do this with the least amount of pain to the poor rooster. The more my father tried to be gentle the more the rooster fought, for I am sure he knew what was coming. It took several attempts trying to get the rooster's neck stretched out on the chopping block before he was put out of his misery. I had witnessed my father being kinder to that rooster than he ever was to us.

Unfortunately for the chickens, and us kids, they would run around the yard without their heads for several minutes before they died. If the axe was wielded incorrectly, the chicken would run around able to squawk without having a head, totally freaking us kids out and giving us nightmares. When old enough, it was my job to remove the feathers from the freshly killed chickens; this was so disgusting. The chicken's nervous system was still active as I tried to pull out its feathers. As kids we had considered these chickens as part of our family. For years we had fed, watered and cleaned their pens. We collected their eggs every day and most of these chickens we had incubated as eggs. These chickens thought of us as their moms. It was very hard for us to eat the chickens.

We also incubated duck and goose eggs. The geese grew up to be fierce and protective of each other and would constantly chase us around and up the apricot trees. If the goose caught one of us it would grab us with its beak and beat us with its massive powerful wings. I spent many hours up in the trees as the geese hissed and danced below, daring me to come down.

Physical work helped us girls release some of our stress and anxiety. As we believed that we were going to grow up to be men, we needed to know how to do men stuff. We mixed concrete, painted rabbit hutches, plowed our field, laid fencing, applied creosote to fence timbers, cleaned the animal pens, all things boys would do. I became quite the tomboy. The neighbor boys and I built a tree house platform in one of our oak trees. The boys loved to have peeing contests off of our tree fort. I proudly proclaimed that if I had a penis, I would win every contest. One boy and I, he was also the oldest in his family, got into a fist fight and when his father found out, he beat him for fighting with a girl and for losing.

I enjoyed spending time with our animals, quietly observing them, as they spent their days foraging and relaxing in the garden. Being with the animals gave me a safe haven. One day my father decided that he wanted me to watch the rabbits as he put the male into each one of the female's cages to mate. In the past, I had observed our animals in the mating process and thought of it as part of nature, but this experience with my father made it seem like a vile and dirty act that he was enjoying. I rightfully feared that he was suggesting that we do the same. Sex, love and childhood were being greatly distorted for me, causing me to try to decipher what was appropriate and what was inappropriate behavior on my father's part.

I never remembered kissing our mother goodnight, but our father demanded a nightly kiss on the cheek. He had quite a heavy beard, and as our tender lips touched his cheek, he would spin his head away from us, burning our lips with his stubble. He got great pleasure in doing this and chided us for falling for his nightly trick. We were so hoping that maybe the next time our goodnight kiss would not hurt. About once a week, during this nightly ritual, he would begin tickling us to the point of tears. As

9

he finished he would then quickly remove our underwear. What
had started out as a harmless game with Dad quickly turned scary.
We were very confused as to why he felt the need to remove our
underwear as our mother looked on in disgust. We did not know
what was expected of us.

The house we grew up in was next door to my
grandparents' house though they sold their house shortly before
my parents bought theirs. The new neighbors had two boys and
one girl. They each had a horse and competed in Gymkhana, a
local horse riding competition. The girl's bedroom walls were
covered in blue ribbons and trophies that she had won. On
weekends the three kids would take their horses for a ten mile ride
up to the lake. When they returned I helped them hose down and
brush their horses. The oldest boy was a year younger than me. He
had a huge white stallion which matched his blonde/white hair. I
had a crush on him but we both were the oldest children in our
families and our similar personalities clashed.

On one occasion he was called into his house to eat his
dinner and to my surprise he let me ride his horse around their
backyard and he asked me to take the horse through the barrel
runs. The horse knew I was afraid of him and refused to do
anything I asked. He insisted on returning to his stall to eat.
Everyone enjoyed watching my smart ass being challenged, and
losing.

The younger boy had a smaller horse, similar to the horses
that Native Americans rode. It was red and white, very stocky and
muscular, like the boy who owned it. This boy told me that I
should do like they do in the movies, get far enough behind the
horse, run up to it, place my hands on its rump and push myself up

onto its back like the Lone Ranger, or maybe it was Tonto. I loved a challenge and I thought I could do anything. He had convinced me that he had done it all the time, though now that I think of it I never did see him do this cowboy trick. I got quite a distance away from the horse and started running. Once I got close enough, I stretched out my arms with hands forward and fingers spread ready to push down and propel myself up. Just then the horse realized what I had in mind. He kicked me full force in the stomach, sending me flying up into the air and dropping down on my butt. Everyone was laughing at me as I sat there bruised. That horse kicked me really hard but I think my pride was hurt the most. It was a miracle I survived all the shenanigans I got myself into. I tried very hard to be the most perfect daughter I could so that nothing else bad would happen to me. I truly believed I could accomplish this. I did not want to be a damaged child.

These same next-door neighbors were best friends with Johnny Cash who, with his wife and four daughters, lived across the river and down a ways from us. His daughters and we four girls were all around the same ages and both our mothers attended the local Catholic Church. Every Sunday our mothers would each dress their four daughters and drive them to Mass. The eight of us girls would sit in the front pews dressed in our little white dresses.

When their father was next door visiting, we would listen to the adults talk about his adventures. On our neighbors' son's birthday, we all piled into the back of their station wagon and went to the local amusement park located along the river and, as we ate cake and ice cream, Johnny Cash sang us his latest songs. He gave the birthday boy an auto harp so he could learn to play an instrument.

11

On one of the Cash girl's birthday we all went to their house and I got to see the famous black bathroom; everything in the bathroom was black. He had a rec room with pin ball machines that we enjoyed playing. I remember how sad the girl was that her father was not there for her on her birthday. All the girls were sad because Christmas had just passed and all they received was a mailed copy of his latest album. I remember telling myself how fortunate I should feel that my father was home every night. Years later, when I saw the movie "Walk the Line," they showed a likeness of that same house I used to visit.

My parents' best friends also had four children, three boys and one girl. The eight of us kids spent a lot of time together. I was the oldest, so I appointed myself in charge. To us kids, everything was a fort to hide in. We used grape arbors, lean-tos, chicken sheds, tree canopies, and our ravine. If we couldn't find a hideaway, we made one by digging a hole in the ground and covering the opening with plywood. We threw sheets over picnic tables, anything to create a world of our own, just big enough for us. And as curious kids we tried almost everything. We would eat just about any flower, make mud pies and jump out of trees.

As leader, I decided that once we were safely hidden in our fort, off went the clothes, as I was fascinated with the boys' penises. They were tiny, shriveled, pink creatures, barely poking their little heads out between their legs. Every time I saw them it made me have to pee. These penises were not like my father's as his was scary, long, hard, and demanding. By ten years old, I knew that they were made to go inside a woman. Once, some of us older kids made the two youngest pretend to have sex, with no success.

12

Usually we would get bored or scared of getting caught so we got dressed and played other games.

Grandma Jane was an x-ray technician at the County hospital. She was fascinated with flowers and took x-rays of every kind she could find. The results were a beautiful shadowy see-through picture printed on orange paper. It was as though she had captured the very essence and spirit of the flower. We loved looking at these and felt privy to a magical world where everything was transparent. My favorites were the Bearded Irises. The flowers' secrets were revealed in print for all to see and I knew then that I never wanted to be x-rayed, causing my secrets to be revealed. I desperately held onto the belief that, if I kept my secrets well hidden deep within me, I would be safe from them. I had yet to realize, that by sharing then releasing my secrets, I could release my shame healing those broken bits of me. There is a saying "You are only as sick as your secrets"....

Grandma also had books depicting gross diseases from around the world that both horrified and mesmerized us. A lot of the pictures depicted children with awful afflictions and I identified with those children. I believed that they had done something very wrong to have been victims of such physical disasters. Like them, I was not a normal child and believed I must have done something wrong to be molested by my father.

Grandma had a large collection of National Geographic magazines that she was very proud of. One of these magazines showed a native tribe performing their coming of age ritual of climbing steep platforms with ropes tied around their ankles. They would dive headfirst, stopping only inches off the ground. My mother tells me that one day she looked outside and there I was,

13

six years old, standing on the top of the swing set with ropes tied on my ankles poised ready to join the ranks of the initiated. Luckily, she was able to talk me down. I still remember that thrill of the count-down, getting ready for my leap into my initiation of manhood.

My father enjoyed the magazines that contained pictures of bare breasted women. These depictions were very confusing to me as, in my mind they appeared to be in the magazines to provide titillating viewing pleasure to the male half of society. I could tell that my father was enjoying these pictures very much; at a young age I knew it was of a sexual nature. This was done in the presence of us girls, our mother and his mother-in-law, creating even more confusion in my little brain as to the rules and dynamics of sex.

My mother was not fond of her mother and would have preferred to stay away from her. When my mother became pregnant with me at age fourteen, my father was eighteen. Grandma Jane had my father arrested for statutory rape and he had to spend the night in jail. The next day she gave my parents permission to marry. It was my father who insisted that we visit Grandma on average about once a month. Grandma Jane was a very sensual and bawdy woman. She enjoyed wearing sheer see-through blouses over sheer torpedo style bras. Grandma lived at the beach and during the summer she would frequently sunbathe in her carport surrounded by the other apartments wearing just her bra and panties. She was pure blood Irish so she never was able to tan; she would turn red and the next day she would be white again.

We girls loved beach-combing the area across the street from her apartment. Grandma showed us that, when you cracked open the sand dollars we found at the beach, they broke into little bird shapes. We loved going to Grandma's house as there was always new and unusual things to discover but it was disturbing to me how attracted my father was to her in a sexual manner, and I didn't like the sexual tension my father created. We were generations of females damaged by childhood sexual abuse.

Summertime was my favorite time of year. Even though I loved school, I loved the freedom I had on long hot summer days, and we kids would be gone all day on our adventures. A new girl moved into town and she and I decided to explore the train tracks along the river. We waded through the shallow river, hidden by the tall bamboo. We were venturing through the wild jungle alone. We were no longer young girls, but explorers. We watched kingfisher birds dive into the water to capture small fish. We saw coyotes chasing rabbits for lunch. We came across an open field where we stretched out on the dry grass, motionless, waiting for the turkey vultures to come pluck out our dead eyeballs. Late in the afternoon, we became hungry and turned around, heading home. Half an hour later, we were met by our parents. My friend's mother was crying and I thought that something bad had happened and that she had sad news for my friend. Instead, her parents were emotional wrecks, having imagined every horrible scenario possible had happened to their daughter during our outing. Mother told me that my friend's parents had insisted on checking every park bathroom, thinking they would find her dead and mutilated body stuffed into a stall. My friend never came to my house again.

Girl Scouts was one of my most favorite activities. Thanks to our troop leader, we were able to go to the cities and visit behind closed doors the inner workings of many businesses. We visited inside the county newspaper and watched how print came to life.

We visited a radio station where, among other things, we discovered how small the workspaces were as so much information was coming out of such a small place, broadcasted far and wide. We were featured on the local television's children's program. We watched Pepsi being bottled. We were able to travel under the dam of our local lake. I loved being a Girl Scout and earned as many badges as I could to sew on my sash. I enjoyed being away from home, in the safety of our troop leader and the other girls. We camped out a lot, sang songs around campfires and meditated under ancient grand oak trees. These activities reinforced my love of nature and camping, becoming one of my most favored escapes. We felt loved by the town and we even walked in the local parades.

Once I reached junior high, I learned how to play the violin that I took home with me every night. One day, in eighth grade, our Girl Scout troop leader told us we were required to wear our uniform to school that following Wednesday. I was mortified. It was bad enough that I carried around a violin case but to also wear my bright green uniform was more than I could stand. Sadly that was the end of Girl Scouts for me.

Summers were very hot and we had heard of a swimming hole six miles from town up into the mountains. Four or five of us girls rode our Stingray bikes looking forward to swimming in the cold water. On the way we would get hot and thirsty, so we snuck into the orange orchards to steal oranges, leaving a sentry to watch for cars and stay with the bikes. One day it was my turn to watch for cars and as one approached, I yelled "car" and to my horror orange bombs came flying out of the orchard onto my head and into the street, just as the car was passing by. Lucky for me the driver kept on traveling down the road. We then mounted our bikes, with our booty of oranges, and headed for the swimming hole. As we rode, we smashed the oranges on our bikes' handlebar post nut to make a hole in the orange, and then sucked out the orange juice. By the time we got to the swimming hole we were hot, tired and sticky with orange juice and couldn't wait to jump into that deep cool water. I loved that swimming hole and even more so when I found out that my Grandma Jane swam there when she was a girl. As I grew older, the swimming hole I so loved started changing energy and it frightened me. The kids began to drink, do drugs and skinny dip. I was uncomfortable with this new energy surrounding me and my friends. I felt that my boundaries were being invaded and the sexual energy was scary for me.

We kids loved wandering the streets at night and visiting with our friends. During the hot summers, we took our Levis and cut them off to make shorts. They were so short that we had to cut out the pockets. We started embroidering our shorts, competing with one another and displaying our own unique style. We made peasant blouses, embroidering them to match our shorts. I imagined our mothers and grandmothers were horrified at what their embroidery lessons had produced. Once the boys caught on that we could sew, they wanted us to turn their Levis into bell bottoms. We took their pants, opened up the outside seams and inserted triangles of fabric and sewed ribbon along the bottom hem. The bigger the bells the better, as my friend's older brothers loved having us make these for them and we loved showing off our talent. We thought of ourselves as young Fashionistas. We had sewing machines and a TG&Y department store just down the street, where we could buy fabric for as low as three yards for a dollar. We were all wannabe hippies as we were too young for the hippy life yet old enough to dress like them.

Being able to create my own clothes was a freedom that I totally embraced. Fabric was very inexpensive. It was the patterns that were so expensive, so several of us split the cost of a pattern. I enjoyed altering the pattern so that my creation would be a little bit different than theirs. I saw the article of clothing in my head and I wanted it finished that day. Clothes had become, at that time, so unstructured that it made it easy for me to produce a dress, skirt or pair of pants in one day. My favorite was the long skirt which was very easy to make as I was built like a string bean. I would sew a tube with a fold on top, insert elastic, hem the bottom, and I was done.

As a young teenager, sewing my own clothes was a freedom of expression that made me feel unique. It gave me a voice and the means to materialize my creativity. I spent the weekends sewing my newest creation to wear to school on Mondays. One Monday I arrived at the bus stop early before anyone else and was first in line. I was so proud and when the bus arrived I took my first step up onto the stairs, not realizing that I was stepping on my floor- length skirt. As I rose up to take the next step, my knees caught on the skirt and pulled it down to the ground. Another step and I would have walked right out of my skirt. There I stood perched on the bus step, two feet taller than everyone else in line, with my granny-panty butt in everyone's face.

One winter my cousin came to stay with us; he lived in Alaska. His mother was the oldest of my father's siblings. My cousin was two years younger than me and he had been named after my father. We girls had a mini-bike that we loved riding but were only allowed to ride it in our back yard. My father allowed my cousin to ride our mini-bike in the street for hours at a time. I was heartbroken to see my father treating his nephew better than he had treated us girls. There may have been something happening in this young boy's life to cause my father to be so kind to him. I was left feeling, once again, betrayed by my father, feeling that I would never be good enough for him. According to him, I would grow up to be a boy and all of this was very confusing to me. Boundaries seemed to be non-existent; sexual roles were confusing. Was I a girl or a boy? Was it okay for my father to molest me? I had no idea what to do with this information I was receiving and perceiving. I could not tell what was right or wrong.

I developed the habit of exaggerating in order to get attention, be heard, and thought of as knowledgeable. I didn't feel that I had any control of it, and I think I enjoyed it as it made my life so much more interesting, but it also became a source of trouble for me. No one enjoyed my embellished truths, and to make it worse, I adamantly denied that I wasn't being 100% truthful. Along with this, I also had a bit of a "know it all" tone to my behavior. This was reinforced and supported with my audience of three. They'd believe anything I said.

In ninth grade I made best friends with a boy and we both loved to dance and together we attended the school dances. We became great dance and Ping-Pong ball partners, winning most of the competitions. On one rare occasion the school played a slow dance song. I had never slow danced before and was horrible at it. Everyone was watching us and I thought it was because I was so horrible. They were all laughing, not because of my dancing but because my friend had pulled up the back of my mini dress and my underwear was showing. That was the first time I remember being able to laugh at myself.

Ruth and I shared a bedroom where we had twin beds pushed up against opposite walls. We drew an imaginary line down the middle of the room creating our own individual space. Ruth is a very creative person and her side of the room always looked so cute. We were only fifteen months apart in age. She was blond and super cute; she knew how to be feminine and she always looked well put together. When Ruth was four she modeled for a local function. She was the youngest in the group and by far the cutest.

In our bedroom everything was painted white. We weren't allowed to put anything on the walls as that would require forbidden nail holes or tape so the back of the door became our artistic outlet. Since our parents never looked at the back of the door, we got as creative as we could. We used crayons to draw peace signs and write all the popular quotes. We truly enjoyed our little light-filled sanctuary. We had our own radio that delivered the magic of music. We listened to Motown and danced, transporting us to unknown worlds, making us feel safe in our room.

Ruth and I would come up with crazy ideas and dares, many of which we carried out. Our father suffered from constant heartburn and had a large supply of Alka-Seltzer in the bathroom. So, on a dare to each other, we broke a seltzer in half and we each placed our half into our vaginas daring the other to not remove it. The tablets fizzed like crazy and we held them there as long as we could until we couldn't stand it any longer. It was fun to be able to explore our bodies on our own and to have each other to share these intimate moments with. It was exciting and yet innocent. In our waking hours, we were competitive and jealous of each other but at night we were best of friends.

At age seven my father started coming to my bed during the night, long after I had fallen asleep. He woke me by telling me to take off my pajamas. He would then rub his fingers on my little clitoris. Mentally I tried to escape through the roof so that I would not feel what he was doing to me. My father would become frustrated that I was not responding to his touch. "Doesn't that feel good?" he'd say "Don't you feel that?" I remained silent, refusing to connect with my body, refusing to feel what he was doing to me. I learned to numb myself. I surrounded my body with a vibration that blurred my reality, I became out of focus. I would keep my eyes shut as tight as possible, clinch my jaw, creating a humming sound in my ears to block out what he was saying. I held my breath and refused to allow my brain to talk to me. I told myself that it would be over soon, he would leave, and I could try to go back to sleep.

Most mornings, I awoke with my hands inside my underwear and my fingers inside my vagina. I was trying to protect myself the best way I knew how and it was comforting to me to sleep like that. On some level, I knew this was not normal and that I could not keep my father from touching me. I was now suffering from vaginal yeast infections and my fingernails would be crusty and yeasty smelling. I would lay there wondering how I would ever grow up to be married and sleep with a man if I was always sleeping with my hands inside myself. I was convinced that I was doomed to live alone with no husband or kids.

I awoke one glorious morning, my hands were not in my underwear and I had no memory of my father coming to my bed. I believed that the incest had stopped, that I would be free from his constant abuse. I lay there in bliss, planning on how my life would be now that things had changed. Now I could sleep without having to protect my vagina from intrusion. I dreamt of being normal, having a husband and kids. I lay there for minutes, enjoying this sweetness. I arose and to my horror I realized that I was naked. My hands were not in my underwear as I was not wearing any. My father had come into my room and I did not remember it. Apparently, I had created ways to escape being present during the abuse and the realization that it could happen to me without me knowing it was devastating. After that I have never in my life been able to sleep naked.

I was turning fifteen during the sexual revolution of 1969. My father's job took us to Mammoth Lakes for six months where they were to build the new road into town. My best friend's little sister was also Ruth's best friend and her father also worked for the same company and we all moved to Mammoth Lakes. My parents rented a Swiss Chalet type ski house and my friend's family camped out along the river. There was so much to see and do. Every weekend our parents took us to see the amazing sights in the mountains. We explored Devils Post Pile, the San Andreas Fault, and places where the Indians had once lived. We dug up hundreds of flint arrowheads, rode the Gondola to the top of Mammoth Mountain, and tried our hand at snow skiing. During the summer, we were free to explore. Ruth and I, and our two friends, had the time of our lives as we hiked and fished the rivers. That summer the Boy Scouts Jamboree was held at one of the lakes. There were thousands of boys arriving daily as we sat on the rocks waving to the buses as they drove by. We met lots of boys and the other three girls enjoyed flirting and kissing with them. I enjoyed spending time with the boys but I was too afraid to be kissing them. We still refer to that time in our life as the "Summer of Fun."

In tenth grade, I got up the nerve to ask my Biology class partner to a Backwards Dance. I had a crush on him and I loved to dance. I went shopping at the mall and managed to buy a dress that was not at all flattering on me. He bought a lovely corsage for me that I managed to pin on my dress right in the middle of my right boob. I picked a buffet type restaurant for our pre-dance dinner and we were totally out of place in our fancy dance clothes and corsage. I was nervous the whole time, so much so that I felt like a failure on my first date and I don't even remember dancing.

The summer of my sixteenth year my parents took Ruth and I and several of our friends camping at the lake. They brought the camper, set it up, and left us there on our own. We were ecstatic. We hiked all the trails, cooked our own food and made nightly campfires. We met other groups of kids also camping out. We made French toast breakfast for our favorite group of boys. We ran wild and more than one Porta-Potty was turned over. All the girls paired up with a boy and for the first time I allowed a boy to kiss me. He told me I needed to open my mouth; when I did, his tongue was racing around and I had no idea what to do and he asked me if there was anything wrong. I had no clue how to kiss so I told him no. My first kiss was disastrous and the next day when he saw me he stepped back in surprise and exclaimed "You're a redhead!"

When I later told my friends about the kiss they all laughed, even Ruth knew how to kiss, and they then explained to me the correct technique.

The next time we went camping, my girlfriend stayed overnight in a boy's tent. Early that morning her parents arrived, excited to tell us about the plane that had crashed into their neighbors' house and that her dad was on the radio, but she was not there. That's when our parents decided we could no longer go camping on our own. The lake also changed their rules and no longer allowed minors to camp alone. I am sure we had something to do with that.

Most Thanksgivings and Christmas's were spent at our house with my father's side of the family joining us. The street out front was perfect for tossing balls, throwing Frisbees and riding bikes. One of my dad's favorite gags was to have me go in the street telling me to run for a pass. As I was running, he would lob the football at an unmarked target in the middle of my back. He threw it with force and when it connected it hurt. He thought this was hilarious and loved pointing out how stupid I was to fall for it every year. Every year I thought I could complete the pass if I just ran faster, tried harder, and was smarter. Little did I realize that this was not his plan; it seemed that he was always looking for ways to make me look stupid.

At these gatherings I was always the oldest cousin. It was my job to watch the younger kids and get my uncles their beers from the fridge while they lay on the couch watching the football games. I was thrilled the year that my Uncle John's best friend came with his two step- daughters. One daughter was my age and the other was one year older. The girls were beautiful and I knew the youngest from high school. She was very sophisticated and mature. They shaved their legs, wore make up, and did up their hair, all of which were foreign to me as they were city girls and I was a farm girl. In our back yard we had a volleyball court, and after our meal, we all gathered for the holiday volleyball game. I was athletic and was excited to show off my abilities. Everyone gathered around to watch the game, though I think the two girls were the main attraction. I was on my dad's team and they were on my uncle's team. I was determined to prove to my dad that I was capable, an asset to his team and something he could be proud of.

The game started out great and we were having lots of fun with everyone trying their best and I had a pretty decent serve. As we rotated positions, I wound up near the net. The ball came over the net and was aimed right at me. My dad yelled for me to set it up so that he could spike it over the net. As the ball came closer, I connected with it poorly and, instead of going upwards, the ball went left, away from my father, out of the court. My father was furious. He stormed over to me, as everyone watched him draw back his right arm, clinch his fist and slug me in the chest telling me to get out of the game. I was horrified and humiliated. Afterwards, I shunned these girls. I was unable to talk with them and would avoid them at school and family gatherings. It was not until thirty-five years later at my cousin's funeral, that I was able to reunite with them putting that shame behind me.

One of my major survival coping skills was "denial." I was the first-born, born into the role of the "Hero" child. I pushed away any knowledge of abuse and was so deep into denial that I believed that I had had the perfect childhood. We always had food, clothes, shelter, we took vacations and my father had a good job. My sister

Ruth had at one time complained to me how bad our mother was and I chewed her head off for saying such a thing. What did she expect when a woman has four daughters, nearly all while in her teens? I exclaimed that we had a good life and she should shut up and quit complaining. I was once again playing my role and she played hers as she was the child that acted out all the family dysfunction.

Ruth was identified as our family "problem" her entire childhood and into adulthood. Discussions centered on her, her problems and what we needed to do to fix her. My family never looked at its own dynamics, only on this problem child. When she had run away at fourteen, I had taken a picture of her and went from neighborhood to neighborhood looking for her. My father followed in the car furious that she had disobeyed him. She was gone for a week. She was only two grades behind me, and I thought I knew all her friends but I did not have a clue as to where she was or whom she was with. She did not discuss her plan with me and I felt helpless. After a week, the police found her and called my parents to see what they wanted to do with her. My parents asked me (I was sixteen at the time) what they should do. Being the dutiful child I said to have her locked up in Juvenile Hall. There she remained for two months and I don't remember us discussing her at all during that time, nor did we visit her. She was removed from our lives, not our problem any longer. It felt as though my parents were happy to leave her there indefinitely. At the end of two months, my parents received a bill from the County charging them for Ruth's room and board. My parents were furious and immediately my mother and I picked her up and brought her home.

26

Ruth had been assigned a social worker, and before they released her, they interviewed me. The social worker told me that based on my parents', Ruth's and my interviews she came to the conclusion that my parents were overly strict, unkind and not nurturing parents. This was the first time I had been confronted with the fact that my parents were something contrary to what I believed about them. The County could not do anything about our situation, as there was no evidence of violence or abuse. I did read in the paper that my father had taken the County to court for charging him for Ruth's care, but he lost the case. The discussion with the caseworker was filed away in the very back of my brain to be ignored. Ruth was the problem in our family and that is just the way it is, at least that is what we told ourselves.

During my senior year, a local shop-owner offered to drive me home from the school bus stop which was two blocks from my house. I did not like this man and I refused his offer. He then pushed me into his car, slammed the door shut and drove off in the direction away from my house. When I realized that he was not taking me home, I opened the front passenger door and attempted to jump out. He grabbed hold of my hair and pulled me back into the car, and closed the door. I began to panic and decided that I was going to get out of that car by any way possible. Once again I opened the door and this time I managed to jump out of the car, landing hard on the pavement. The car behind us stopped to help and to my good fortune the driver of that car was a family friend and also a Sheriff's Deputy. He took me home and called his office. I was interviewed and the man was arrested.

The next day, it was reported in the local newspaper, though my name was not mentioned. My Grandma Jane saw the article in the paper and called to warn me about a girl my age being kidnapped. When I told her that it was me she comforted me over the phone. No one else, besides her and my parents, knew of this incident. My parents treated me as if I had caused this to happen to myself. They offered me no comfort or support. I was required to go to the District Attorney's office for questioning and I went alone, as my parents wanted nothing to do with this.

I never felt or heard pride from my parents, though my mother did express pride in that she had us so well trained. She told her friends how she could leave us in the doctor's waiting room, then come out to find the nurse saying how very well behaved we were. Like monkeys in a circus we were beat, slapped and threatened into being as quiet and inconspicuous as possible. Knowing what I know about my Grandma Jane's history, along with my mother's childhood, it explains a lot.

A dear wise woman once told me a magical story about what happens when we are being created as female babies. When in their mother's womb, their bodies are creating the only eggs they will ever have to create new life. These eggs are created in the baby's womb, as the baby is being created in the mother's womb. Essentially, mother and baby are jointly creating the next generation. This means that I, as an egg in my mother's womb, was created in my Grandma Jane's womb. I had begun life inside my redheaded, blue-eyed, left-handed grandma.

I did not have any adults in my life that openly expressed love towards me except for my grandma. I don't recall being held, hugged, cuddled, kissed or touched in a loving manner. My Grandma Jane was the closest thing to attachment that I felt. When she would visit us, she would stop at the local hamburger shop to get four, eight if our friends were visiting, soft serve ice-cream cones. There she would appear on our front porch ringing the doorbell with ice cream dripping down her arms as us kids squealed with delight. On one of the few birthdays of mine that she remembered, she bought me a purple eight foot long stuffed toy snake. She stopped close to our house, in front of the fire department, and threaded the snake down the back of her clothing. When she rang our door bell, there she stood with this huge snake head peering at me over her shoulder. She may have not been a good mother, but she tried to be a good grandmother.

When I turned seventeen, my parents bought me my paternal grandmother, Grandma Lee's used car. I so enjoyed the freedom my little car gave me and I took every chance I could to drive her around. I was allowed to drive to school two days a week and I would fit as many friends as I could into my little car. On the way to school, I would stop at the beach and drive in circles in the sand, throwing us all against the sides of the car as we laughed and screamed. The first time I tried this, it was so much fun we were almost late getting to school. As I parked in the school parking lot, we began to rush down the hill to our classes when I noticed that all the hubcaps were missing on my wheels. I had to speed back to the beach, find all four, place them securely on my tires, and then rush back to school again.

Saturdays, I would drive across town to visit with my girlfriends. I would gather up as many friends as I could find. We would drive to the only stop light in town and as the light turned red I would crank up the radio. We would then all jump out of the car dancing until the light turned green again. One Saturday, I decided to let my girlfriend practice driving my car. As we were driving around our neighborhood, her at the wheel, we turned the corner and there in the middle of the road stood my parents. I was in big trouble. They told me to drive my friend home, drive myself home and place my keys on the kitchen counter, where they would remain for one month.

One week later, my father whispered in my ear to come to his bedroom with him. He told me to take off my clothes and to masturbate him while he fondled my breasts. After he ejaculated, he handed me my car keys as a reward. The incest had now gone to another level. My father was making it look like it was to my advantage to participate with him. I felt dirty and disgusted. I felt like a whore. I knew in reality that I didn't have a choice, yet I was made to feel like we were partners.

Years before, my father had removed our street mailbox and rented a PO Box, so that we girls could not receive mail. I don't know what precipitated in him doing this but I do know that he blamed us for having to take such drastic actions. Only he had access to the combination of the PO Box. After one of his molestations, he handed me the combination numbers to the box and told me to never tell my mother. Not only was I now a part of this liaison, he was pitting me against my mother. He was now treating me as his mistress and I knew that I had to get out of his house as soon as possible.

To my surprise, my sensuality did not feel as damaged or threatened as much as my sexuality had. I enjoyed my changing body though it felt like the rest of the world was somehow threatened by my sensuality. I remember my mother telling us girls that any skin we exposed gave others permission to touch it. It was confusing to have my parents strictly monitoring my clothing, makeup and attitude. I was shamed and humiliated by the choices I made, the styles I enjoyed and the dancing that set me free. I was told that the outside world was a horrible, bad place. When in reality the horribleness was in my own house, in my own bed, caused by my own father.

One day my sensuality betrayed me. I was in my room when I became very sexually aroused and my body was demanding attention. I wanted so badly for my father to come to my room. My body was becoming my father's. Puberty had finally created sensations within me that I had never felt before. Some studies have shown that young girls' bodies that are subjected to sexuality at a young age develop sooner than nature intended. I was a very skinny girl who grew huge breasts. Now I understood what my father wanted. He wanted me to want his attentions and he wanted me to be his sexual partner. He didn't come into my room that day and I am so very thankful that I did not receive sexually pleasing gratification from him.

When I was a senior in high school, I worked on the weekends at a local restaurant and my parents started charging me rent. During this time, I suffered with recurring tonsillitis, eight times in six months. Over the Christmas vacation, I was hospitalized and had my tonsils removed. My father's insurance covered the surgery, but not the anesthesiologist and my parents made me pay that doctor's bill. This was a sign to me that my parents were through with me. They were not willing to provide for me once I graduated from high school and that I needed to start planning for my future.

SOULTHRIVER

CHAPTER TWO

Even though in the past, I had had crushes on boys I was still afraid of them, the nice ones at least. This explains my attraction to Jack. It was the summer before twelfth grade when we met. My girlfriend's parents had a cool Thunderbird car with suicide doors. We both had a death wish and she did eventually die driving her sports car. Her parents let her drive their fancy car around town and she loved to burn rubber and drive fast downhill and several times she was able to get all four tires off the ground.

Eventually, the neighbors called the police ending our crazy fun but before that she and I had picked up a guy we had seen around town who was visiting from the next town over. He was dressed like a cowboy, complete with hat, belt, Levis and boots. He wasn't the loose hippy type that scared me, he was the Marlboro man. He was dark, sullen and I was hooked. He was demanding and aggressive and I felt safe with that and his demanding ways excited me. He was rough and forceful. My hair was very long and he used it to get what he wanted. He would grab my hair, yanking me towards him, and pulling me down to sit by him. I had made the choice to be with him and it made me feel powerful and in control of my body. I gave myself entirely over to him. I knew that my parents would not like him and that pleased me.

This was a new feeling for me and very distant from the life I had at home. It felt daring and brave to be involved with such as intense, violent and demanding person. I released all my sexual frustrations, confusions and desires to him. I was a natural at pleasing him. I kissed with such intensity as I felt my body responding to him. I enjoyed performing oral sex on him, believing that he was being vulnerable and that I was in charge. I was enjoying being wanted by him and I was consumed with pleasing him.

That following December, he enlisted in the Air Force. When he was in basic training and technical school he would call me from the Base phone, long distance, and we would talk for hours. During that time I believe that I was becoming unconsciously nervous about graduating high school. My parents had told us girls that their job was to put a roof over our heads, to feed and clothe us and, once we graduated from high school, their job was done and we would be on our own. I had done well in school and was earning my own money by working on the weekends but I couldn't see how I could support myself and, on some level, believed that Jack would be my answer. I so desperately wanted to leave my parents' house and I didn't believe that I could do it on my own.

One night as I was being consumed with anxiety about my future I prayed and prayed, then demanded, that God do something. As I sat on my bed crying and worrying, a large bright yellow glowing ball appeared in my room and swirled around me getting larger and larger until I was contained within this golden sphere. I felt as if I was being visited by a spirit, possibly by God. It lasted for maybe a minute and I felt a peace come over me and a connection to something outside of my current life. Within days, Jack proposed.

In March of that year, Jack received transfer orders to England and we were married that May, one month before my high school graduation. Neither of our parents liked the idea of us getting married. Because I was only seventeen years old, I needed to get permission from the County to be allowed to marry, and during the interview, I insisted that this was what I wanted. The preacher who married us also interviewed us to make sure we wanted to do this. I was adamant that this was what I wanted. I was sure that this would be the answer to all my problems even though I am not sure I liked, let alone loved, Jack. I organized and paid for our wedding. Jack arrived two days before the wedding and wore his military uniform to our ceremony.

Ruth was sixteen years old and seven months' pregnant. My father had forbidden her to come to my wedding. It broke my heart to not have her there with me. She was young, unwed and pregnant, just like my mother had been with me. Our father had absolutely no compassion, understanding or love for her or her situation. The father of her unborn child was twenty-one and refused to have anything to do with her. My parents had her placed into foster care with strangers and covertly she and I had maintained contact. I was so ashamed that my father completely dominated my life, to the point of dictating who could attend my own wedding. It never occurred to me to challenge him or to ever go against his wishes.

We had our wedding reception at the church hall and, when it was over, Jack and I went to the small guest house on Jack's parents' property where we would live until he left for England one month later. I was still wearing my wedding dress, high with anticipation of my new life, when Jack decided to teach me how to use a rope to lasso him. Maybe he saw this as a newly-married cowboy couple gesture. I was excited to have him teach me something new, as this sounded like a wonderful ritual to start out our new life together. He demonstrated how to create a slipknot, swing it over my head allowing the loop to get bigger and bigger until it was big enough to go over his head and body. I was swinging the rope over my head as he began running from side to side. The loop became just the right size and I tossed the rope, which slipped over his head falling down to his ankles. I pulled the rope tight like I had seen on television. Unfortunately, I pulled too hard and he fell onto the ground. He was furious and decided I needed to learn a lesson. He made me run in my floor-length wedding dress as he lassoed me. Once the rope was around me, he pulled as hard as he could until I was on the ground. With the rope around my ankles, he dragged me to the house. Once in the house, he picked me up, threw me against the wall, and started choking me. I was heart-broken.

This was not how I anticipated celebrating our marriage and my new-found freedom. The type of ritual I thought we were creating was quickly changing into a ritual that would become all too familiar and frequent in my new life. I knew I was in trouble and I felt as though there was no one whom I could turn to for help. I was that little girl who had been told by my mother that anything bad that happened to me was my own fault. I had made the decision to marry Jack so I must live with my decision. I felt all alone and terrified that I was going to be moving very far away. I had really screwed up this time and I was not able to get myself out of this situation. I was fucked. I decided to convince myself that I would create new coping skills to deal with what I was going to be experiencing behind closed doors, in my new life, one I had chosen.....for life. Years later, I showed my solemn wedding pictures to my therapist who said that my groom looked like the violent men he had treated in prison.

Two months later, I arrived in England. When I arrived Jack told me that he was in a mandated drug program. His drug abuse had caused him to be transferred already to two different positions on the Base. Unfortunately for me, the only time Jack was a nice guy was when he was drunk or high. Yet I was determined to make the most of my new life, grateful that I no longer lived in fear of my father molesting me. I was free from my father and I was convinced that I could create a wonderful new life in a new country, with my new name and my new husband.

We lived in a flat on the top floor of a three-story building that had started out as a school, later became a brothel and eventually an apartment building which was scheduled to be razed soon. Our heating was what is now called on-demand. There were meters on the tanks used to heat the bathwater, the kitchen sink water, the bedroom and the stove/oven. All of these meters required coins to operate. It was cold and damp that winter and each room was separated from the other opening out to the hallway. We had half the rooms upstairs, another couple had the other half, and we shared a bathroom. When I frequently ran out of coins I used the electrical box punch-outs that were all over the new construction area next door. The punch outs were the perfect shape, allowing me to have lots of hot water, heat in the bedroom and flame to cook our meals with. I was proud of my ingenuity and new success at running our new household. I did this without even thinking that it was my landlord who would be collecting the money, not some utility fairy. I was so embarrassed when my landlord chastised me for cheating him.

Our neighbors were a very sweet couple who were about ten years older than us and I really enjoyed spending time with them. They had a television and we watched the Olympics together. They were very helpful in my adjustment period in this foreign country. They were very kind and gentle with each other and with me. They both worked so I was home alone most of the time. I know my neighbors must have heard Jack yelling and beating me. Once, he even tried to throw me down the stairs over the hand rail. I frequently wore black eyes and bruises on my skin. The neighbors and I never spoke about what went on in our half of the apartment. The three of us were being terrorized by this crazy man I had married. We were all grateful that he was gone most of the time.

Our apartment was seventy-five dollars a month furnished, complete with a horse-hair mattress. I tried to create the wife role I was now in and went to the local grocery store to stock up my new kitchen. Walking the isles of the market, I began to notice the difference in my new surroundings. Food items in England came in much smaller quantities and most people frequented the market on a daily basis. The advantages were that bread came warm in packages of four slices, eggs were sold by the half dozen and milk came in pints. I was shopping for a two-week supply, while everyone else was doing their daily visit. I brought my huge amount of items to the register and watched as the groceries piled up. It was then I realized what the cute wicker baskets people brought to the store were for. Luckily for me, they sold me some paper bags. I later bought cloth bags and have used them ever since.

Jack stayed away a lot, only coming home to sleep, claiming that he had to work seven days a week. We joked that he needed to bring home a note from his boss explaining why he was away from home all the time. I never did figure out what he was doing when he wasn't at work. It was a gloomy cold winter and I was alone most of the time but I told myself over and over that this was surely better than being molested by my father.

Two months later, we moved into a cute little brick house in a small village and our family increased to three, with the addition of a black and white kitten. We now owned a little green car. Our next door neighbors were a darling family and he too was in the Air Force, living in an identical brick house and yard like ours. He was a young, tall, gentle, giant. She was a tiny woman from Mexico, and they had a newborn baby girl. We spent many evenings and weekends together, along with several other Air Force couples. She taught me how to make Mexican food from scratch and she had brought her own tortilla press from home.

Jack and I spent our first Christmas together at our neighbor's house and several mutual friends joined us. My contribution was to cook the turkey and I bought the biggest I could find, forgetting how small my oven was. I rubbed butter all over this huge turkey, placed it in an aluminum basin and, with the help of the butter coating, I literally shoved it into the oven. The door wouldn't close but I assumed that there would be no problems with me leaving it open a bit. I turned on the flame and went to bed. When I awoke the next morning, the kitchen was full of smoke. I was sure the turkey was ruined. But as it turned out the turkey was broasted with a crispy coating and everyone said it was the best turkey they ever had.

I began working on Base at the Base Exchange in the cashier's cage where I cashed checks, counted money, and balanced the registers of all the businesses on Base. After six months, I was promoted to maintaining and stocking the candy, cigarettes and body products section of the Exchange. Working there was lots of fun. Mondays we were closed and it was also our stock day. We collected our stock replacements from the delivery truck, cleaned and restocked our shelves, while dancing in our isles. The English women that I worked with were children during WWII and shared their horror stories of bombings, food rationing, and staying in fallout shelters. Work became my refuge; much like school had been when I was a child. Being with these women helped me keep sane and freed me to be young and playful. Life with Jack was causing me great unhappiness and I began to plan a way out. I knew that I needed to change the way I saw my future if I wanted a better life.

On the weekends, Jack and I would drive through the countryside, enjoying the rolling hills and college towns. The setting was beautiful and peaceful outside but inside the car, Jack was like a time bomb and I never knew when he would explode. Invariably something I said would set him off. He would begin punching the steering wheel, the dashboard and then my face, all as he was driving seventy miles per hour down the road. Several items in the car became damaged or broken, along with my spirit and body. Doors could no longer stay closed on their own, knobs no longer worked and windows were shattered. On one of these occasions, we were parked on the military Base and Jack was punching me in the face and bashing my head against the window when a Military Policeman approached and told him to take me off

Base to do that. This once again reinforced that deep subconscious belief I had that I was bad, deserving to be treated as such. Yet a voice inside me said I was strong and deserved to be happy.

Telephone service was very expensive at that time, a call to the states started at twenty dollars and there was limited access to outside lines. On Mother's Day, it was necessary to call the operator and be placed on the list of available times for outside calls. Mail was delivered twice a day and I wrote a few letters to my mother and sisters. I received a letter from my sister Jean and one from my Grandma Lee but that is all the contact I can remember having with my family during the two years that I lived overseas.

Once again, I was living with a horrible secret that kept me isolated and shallow. I was suffering physical injuries at the hands of Jack and I lied about their origins. The day following a beating, Jack would see my bruises and lumps and ask me what had happened to me. He would try to appear confused and a little remorseful as to what had happened, yet detaching himself from the awful truth. In the midst of this, I began to grow stronger and more determined to recapture the wonderful person I was meant to be.

A year had passed and our life together eventually escalated to the point that Jack did not want me there any longer and was sending me back to California. I was elated! I couldn't believe my luck. I held my breath for days, awaiting my departure. I avoided eye contact with him so he couldn't see the hope in my eyes. I was walking on egg shells, praying that this wasn't a dream and that this was really going to happen. It was such a challenge to keep my joy hidden and I couldn't believe my luck. I was finally getting out of this hell. I was so miserable that I was even looking forward to being back at my parents' house.

On that much anticipated day we safely arrived at Heathrow Airport, London. A friend who was familiar with the area drove us to the airport. My heart was pounding and I was shaking inside. We waited for my flight as I struggled to keep calm. Jack saw my leaving as a form of punishment and I knew that, if I let on in any way at all that I was happy to be leaving, he would blow up. Our friend and Jack spent the waiting time in conversation. This was the early 1970's and I occupied myself by watching all the interesting looking people from around the world coming and going. It was an exciting time to be in England and I so wished I could have enjoyed it.

As we waited for my plane, word came over the public announcement system that the baggage handlers had gone on strike. Strikes were a common occurrence in England at that time. No planes would be leaving. I went weak, I nearly fainted, I gathered up my luggage and like a zombie I walked back to our car for the long drive home. I felt abandoned by God and the Universe. I couldn't even leave the country. Luckily Jack's friend was with us, protecting me from Jack's wrath. Deep down, I knew that I was not finished fighting for my life. I knew I needed to get stronger and stronger with the determination needed to get myself out of this situation.

When Jack informed me that he was going to send me to California, it allowed me only two days to give notice at work. Jack worked with my boss's husband, so when we returned from the airport, they arranged for me to get my old job back. By then, I had had years of training and experience on how to push my feelings very deep down inside me. I knew how to continue on with life as if nothing had happened. In order to keep everything pushed down, I took a second job at night, working at the pizza place on Base. Work was my escape; if I wasn't at work, I was home sleeping.

Before my new job, I had never even eaten a pizza. My boss taught me how to toss dough into the air, catch it, and toss it again until I had a nice round crust. Most of our late evening customers were F4 fighter pilots returning from bombing missions in Viet Nam. Against regulations and their safety, the pilots wore their flight uniforms to dinner. They talked about flying upside down over the ocean seeing who could get their cockpit closest to the water. They too were experiencing horrible events in their lives, making my predicament, in my mind, pale in comparison.

The two years we lived in England, we never traveled off the island. There was much happening around us, such as the trouble with the 1972 Olympics, the IRA bombings in London, Viet Nam war, and the Iranians were placing bombs on our Base, not that I felt safe at home.

During the two years we were in England, Jack had three nervous breakdowns and was admitted to the psych ward each time. I dutifully visited him and he appeared to be medicated and always engrossed in some craft project, much like what you would see on television when they depicted a mental ward. I was not consulted or advised as to his condition, necessary medication, or his diagnosis. He was property of the military and I was intentionally left out of the discussions. Upon release from his third episode close to the end of his two-year tour, the doctor at the mental ward released him back to work. The doctors said that they were done with him and that it was up to me to take care of him.

Driving to one of his follow-up visits with the doctors, Jack dropped me off at one of the Base recreation rooms. It was during working hours and I was the only one there. As I was walking around the room looking for something to read, I came across a pile of photographs and began looking through them. To my horror, they were all pictures of me walking on the Base. All the pictures had been taken from a distance. I was scared. I didn't know what was happening. Why had they been put there? What was the message in them being there? I became very fearful even though I knew there was nothing in those pictures that would cause Jack to be angry with me, I felt fearful for my life. I was being stalked. I didn't know why or by whom, but I did know that Jack had something to do with it. When he picked me up, I did not mention the photos and neither did he; we never did talk about them.

One day Jack brought home a pet rabbit. I really enjoyed having a pet and spent a lot of time with her. We had her only two weeks when Jack discovered that she had chewed a hole in one of his shirts. Jack was so pissed off that he took the bunny outside and, with a sword, he sliced her head off. He left the blood on the sword and would frequently bring it out to show his friends, telling them that he had used it on someone and that was their blood left on the blade.

I was so despondent and feeling hopeless with my life that I took a long kitchen knife and threatened to slice my neck. Jack asked me to please do it and that he wanted to watch me. I decided to not give him the satisfaction and returned the knife to the

84

kitchen drawer. I had made the decision that, through all this, I still wanted to live. I began slowly building up more strength and resolve with each passing day. Over and over, I reminded myself that I did not survive incest to be in this horrible soul-crushing dilemma. I was building thriver genes. I was re-writing my story.

At the end of two years of living in England, Jack was transferred to Ellsworth Air Force Base, South Dakota, just outside of Rapid City. We rented a large farm house out in the country, the site of the family's original homestead. The family had since built a house on the other end of the ranch. We were to be the caretakers of their five thousand acres. Since Jack worked full-time on the Base, I became the caretaker. Jack, true to his ways, seldom came home to our place out in the countryside. I did not have a car or public transportation, so I spent all of my time on the ranch. Alone with myself and nature, I began visualizing the steps necessary towards my goals, allowing myself glimmers of what my future could look like.

I became friends with our landlords and their two adult children who also had houses on the ranch. Our landlord was pioneering "Beefalo" through artificial insemination, using Buffalo sperm to create large cross- bred animals for dairy and meat. I was commandeered to help with the recording of medical information. Weekly, during breeding season, the veterinarian came to check if the heifers had become pregnant and how far along they were. The landlord rounded them up and herded them through a shoot where the vet, and I with my clipboard, checked them. The vet put on one very long glove, covered it with Dawn dishwashing detergent, and inserted his arm into the birth canal. I recorded the heifer's ear tag number, if she was pregnant, and how far along she was. He had all positive results; all the heifers were pregnant. The experiment started off on a positive note.

He was pioneering this new breed and had no idea how large the calves would be, and how large a calf the heifers could deliver. When the anticipated delivery date neared, we had a freak snowstorm when the heifers out in the pasture began giving birth as the snow fell. That night, I was awakened by the owner's son; a heifer had delivered a calf out in the pasture and he needed my help. The calf was not responding to its mother's attempts to get it on its feet. We jumped into his old Ford pickup, shocks long gone, and drove for several minutes in the blinding snow until we finally found the heifer and her calf. The mother was standing next to her baby, who was still lying on the ground. We needed to position ourselves between momma and baby so that we could put the calf in the truck bed. I distracted her as he maneuvered the truck between them. We were able to pick up the hundred-pound calf and safely put it into the truck bed. We then jumped into the truck and drove towards the barn. As we were driving, the mother was ramming the tailgate. He had to do some tricky driving to keep her from ramming the truck doors. We succeeded in getting the calf to the barn, safely into the heated nursery room. I rubbed the calf with a gunnysack, its texture is much like its mothers tongue, and was able to get it to respond eventually, sucking on my finger before we returned it to its mother.

Most of the beefalo calves were too big for their mother's birth canal. The calf's feet would be sticking out of the mother's birth canal, but the rest was too big to pass through, so we had to wrap chains around the calf's feet and pull as hard as we could. It was so heartbreaking to hear the heifers bellowing with pain. We were successful in most cases but, in some cases, the cows had to be loaded into the flatbed truck and taken into town to the vet's office for a caesarean operation. Some heifers suffered terribly and were not able to take care of the newborns. I took these newborns to the heated nursery and rubbed them down and, after they started sucking my fingers, I gave them a bottle of cow's milk. The calves weighed over 100 pounds each and their legs were longer than mine. Most of the calves born were male, not the milking/breeding females they had counted on.

That winter, our landlord rented out the house we were living in to a real ranch hand and his family. We moved into the mobile home that backed up to the pasture where the horses would come down at night for shelter. That was the winter I called "The Winter of the 100's." I awoke one morning shivering under my electric blanket and I hadn't realized that the electricity was off. As I got out of bed, I noticed I could see my breath as I exhaled. I grabbed my Levis from the nightstand and, as I went to put them on, they literally broke in half; they were frozen solid. All along the baseboards, I noticed piles of snow and snow coming in from the electrical outlets. In the bathroom, the water in the toilet bowl, the shampoo, cream rinse and other liquids were frozen solid. The storm had reached 100 mph winds with a chill factor of 100 degrees below zero, creating 100-foot snow drifts, hence "The Winter of the 100's."

Jack went to work as I surveyed the damage and waited for our pipes to defrost. In the meantime, I used the toilet in the cement milking room. Everyone was miserable, the cows, the horses, the barn cats, my cat Tara and my small black-wired hair terrier dog, Jerky. The only thing working in my mobile home was

47

the gas oven, which I turned on, opened the door, sat on the kitchen chair with my cat and dog wrapped in a blanket, and placed my feet on the oven door. The phone was not working and Jack took this opportunity to stay in town as I continued to help with the ranch. Alone once again, I was learning to be self-sufficient, growing more confident in my abilities.

Jack didn't return home, nor did I hear from him, for two months. Easter weekend, my friends from Rapid City came and picked me up. We had a great time watching movies on one of the only three channels available and only if the technician was able to get to work that day. That night was another heavy storm, the next morning the newscast said that the roads were all closed, and they were issuing tickets to those who chose to drive on the highways. This went on for four days. On the fifth day, the storm had passed and Jack called. He was furious. He had driven out to the ranch and found Jerky underneath our mobile home, frozen to death. He was yelling on the phone that I had killed his dog.

When the weather was better I went back to the ranch. Days later, Jack came to make amends and took me to where he had been staying. It was a dark basement apartment with no windows that he shared with two other guys. While we were there, I didn't know what to do with myself as the three of them slumped in their chairs getting high, so I cleaned their mountain of dirty dishes. When stressed or afraid I like to clean, but in doing so, I could see that I was reacting to situations instead of choreographing my life. Washing a bunch of stoners' dishes was the last thing I should be doing.

On one of the occasions that I was left alone out on the ranch, I thought of driving back to California in my huge boat of a car, though I wasn't too confident in its ability to get me there. My father said he would come and we'd drive back together. I am sure it would not have been a delightful father/daughter trip. I truly believe that he had planned a sexual getaway with me. I am so grateful that the trip never happened. It did not happen because I did not let it. I slowly was becoming comfortable with listening to my intuition.

After living on the ranch for one year, we moved to on-Base housing. We lived in a cute little duplex with a front and back yard on a winding, tree-lined street; complete with MP's that patrolled my neighborhood, stopping to tell me that I needed to pull the dandelions out of our front yard. Two years prior, it was okay with the MP's that Jack beat me on Base but now they were threatening to write me up for weeds in my front yard.

I was now working six days a week from 3 am until 3 pm at Control Data manufacturing plant, making computer circuit boards. The factory was perched just above one of the Lakota Sioux reservations. Most of my co-workers lived on the reservation. We didn't really interact with one another, as our work was assembly-line work and we mostly stayed to ourselves during lunch break. I was happy to once again have an escape from my home life. As my employment history improved, I learned that at some point I would financially be able to take care of myself.

By now I had suffered, at the hands of Jack, a bad blow to the head that required several stitches, a broken nose and several black eyes, more beatings than I can remember. There were also sexual attacks and rapes by Jack as he would oftentimes tie me up and use a hammer handle to rape me with. Things were getting worse so, when he stated that I was to join the Air Force, I was

49

elated once again to find a way out. I took the entrance exams and decided on a career in Accounting. The Viet Nam war was winding down, so enlistments were delayed for several months. Jack was not happy that I would not be leaving immediately. I didn't see much of him before I left.

I spent my twenty-first birthday in Basic Training. I was one of the oldest Airmen in our squadron. On one of our get-togethers with the other squadrons, I was surprised to see a woman that I knew from the Base in South Dakota. I had met her and her husband at a party Jack and I had attended. I was happy to see a familiar face and excited to reminisce with her. While talking with her, she pulled out of her pocket a photo strip, the kind you get from a camera booth, of her and Jack. She was very sad and told me that they had wanted to get married but, of course, both of them were already married. Angrily she walked away; I never saw her again.

In Technical Training School, my superiors discovered that I had leadership skills and I was assigned to lead our co-ed Battalion. At 6 am every morning, I drilled our Battalion on the flight line, marching in the winter cold and snow of San Antonio, Texas. During Tech School, I received my Base assignment orders for Misawa, Japan. Jack's four-year enlistment was coming to an end and, with the Viet Nam war ending, anyone with a problematic personnel record was not allowed to re-enlist, which included him. Jack refused to go with me to Japan and wanted me out of the military. He convinced me to apply for an Honorable Hardship Discharge, based on the fact that we could not be lifers together. I was awarded a discharge after being in the military one week short of six months.

50

We were both civilians now and decided to move back to our hometown. Life with Jack only got worse. I hid from my family and friends what was happening to me. I again immersed myself into work. I found a good job where I felt appreciated and compensated for my efforts. I felt like part of a team. I worked ten-hour days, six days a week. Even though I was the youngest in our department, I was given the top jobs.

I hated showing up to work with black eyes. I lied about what was happening and everyone knew I was lying. My perception of a battered wife was that of a woman who was uneducated, a slob, a bitch, low class, deserving of such abuse, stupid for not only putting up with it, but also staying with the batterer. I was horrified for anyone to find out that I was a battered wife. It was so shameful. I was unable to reach out for help and was unaware of the type of services available to me. Like the sexual abuse, I once again felt I was to blame for the awful things that were happening to me. I felt strong and capable at work, yet weak, defenseless and less-than at home.

The company I worked for shut down every year for two weeks in July. During one of these vacations, Jack and I attended a BBQ at a friend's house. We were all sitting in the living room having a lively discussion; I don't remember the topic. Unknowingly, I said something that Jack didn't like so he hit me, breaking my jaw. The other guests told him to take me home. I didn't seek medical treatment. I was unable to open my mouth, though I could drink fluids through a straw and smoke my cigarettes. This lasted for the remainder of my two-week vacation. I stayed away from friends and family until my jaw healed.

I couldn't believe that I was with him. My self-worth and self-esteem were non-existent. I was beaten down, ensnared in the victim role. I was certain that my escape would come with my death by his hands. I knew I had to do something, as I was certain that I was not born to live this hell. I was NOT the incest; I was NOT the abusive marriage. I was more than that.

While we were living in South Dakota, my sister Ruth and her two-and-a-half-year-old son Sean visited with us. During her visit, Jack put on an act as a caring, loving husband, brother-in-law and uncle. Ruth was in a new relationship and thought it would be a good idea for us to take Sean and raise him. I knew this was a bad idea for Sean. Jack was not a nice man, and I thought Ruth needed to give her new relationship time. I told her to wait things out as she was not yet eighteen and I had hoped she would feel differently as time went on.

A year and a half had passed and we were once again living in California. Ruth was in the same relationship and Sean was now four years old. During a small dinner party, she and I were sitting on the floor having a lovely conversation. Sean was sitting in her lap when, out of the blue, she asked me to take Sean. Apparently she had given this much thought and, along with her boyfriend, decided that it was best for Sean to live with us. She had asked me as Sean sat in her lap. My heart started to pound and my senses went haywire, my adrenaline was pumping, I needed to think fast and do the right thing. I told her yes, I would take him and I would take him that minute. I told her to gather up his things and that he was coming home with me.

It was a very sad and traumatic situation, especially for Sean. We spent the first couple of days crying and sleeping as I tried to answer all his questions. How can you give a child away? Why can't he choose who he lives with? Over and over, he asked me these questions. It was heartbreaking to see a child experience rejection from his mother. I knew how Ruth was raised, as I had witnessed the dislike in my mother's eyes when she looked at her. I understood why Ruth lacked the "natural" mother's instinct. I truly understood her choice and that it was best for Sean, but Sean had no way of understanding what was happening to him.

I believe, as others in my family did, that Sean would not be alive if I hadn't taken him. Even though he was my sister's son and already part of my family, I felt it very important that Jack and I make ourselves his legal parents. We hired a lawyer and began the adoption process. During the waiting period, Jack began to be violent with Sean. At first it was verbal abuse, then inappropriate demands and finally physical abuse. I had decided early in life that I was not going to have children, as I did not feel that children were safe in this world and I couldn't stand to see a child suffer. So when the Universe brought me Sean, I felt very accountable as to how I took care of this precious being. I subconsciously began planning my and Sean's escape from this situation. This was my first step towards breaking the family line of really bad mothers and abusive and incestuous fathers. I became stronger in my will to live by protecting this wonderful gift that had been given to me.

On my monthly trip to the bank to make my car payment, the teller told me that just that morning Jack had come in and withdrew all our money and told her that he was going to buy a gun. When I called him at work to tell him that we needed that money to make the car payment, his boss told me he hadn't worked there in five weeks. When Jack finally did show up at home, he had a brand new forty five pistol and was riding a motorcycle that he had traded in his six-month-old car for. He proudly showed the motorcycle to a friend who noticed that the serial numbers on frame did not match the engine or the DMV paperwork, meaning that it was stolen. This meant that we had lost all the money we had paid on the car and now still owed on the balance. Jack then informed me that he was hanging out at the Hell's Angels Clubhouse as a prospect, someone who was hoping to become part of the club.

Jack threw a party at our house to show off his new pistol and motorcycle. The party seemed to be going well and we were all sitting around having just finished our dinner. We were all talking, laughing, and telling jokes. All of a sudden Jack pulled out his pistol and put it to my head. His friends tried to calm him down, but no one moved a muscle; they were all afraid of him. I don't remember just how it happened, but eventually he did calm down and everyone quietly left.

This wasn't to be the only time he pulled a gun on me. Jack, Sean, and I were driving downtown when he began to berate Sean, telling him what a fuck-up he was. I gathered up my strength and, as Jack stopped the car at the next stoplight, I managed to climb out of my seat and into his. I was in such a fury. I was an angry mom who needed to take care of her child. Jack opened his car door, got out of the car and ran to the trunk. He pulled out a shotgun and aimed it at me. I jumped out of the car and raced towards him, demanding that he do it, just go ahead and shoot me. By this time, there was traffic gathering around us as people stopped to watch the drama take place. Jack hurriedly put the gun away, pushed me into the car and drove home. I had put on my

Warrioress armor and fought the dragon. No longer would I accept or tolerate beatings, rapes, abuse. I was feeling my new-found power.

That was the changing point in our marriage. With my new-found power, I knew that I needed to end this horrible union. He must have felt that something inside me had snapped and that I would never be the same. He had decided that, in order to gain full control over Sean and me, it was necessary to move us to the other end of California where his parents lived. The next day while I was away at work, he put Sean on the front of his motorcycle for a ten-hour ride to his parents' house. He had called me at work when he was halfway there and said that, if I didn't follow him, he would kidnap my parents, place them in the trunk of my car and kill them. Several hours later, he called again saying that he had dropped Sean off at his parents' house, and then rode his motorcycle into town. On the way back to his parents' house, the front tire came off. I was so upset at what could have happened had Sean been on the front of the bike as they sped along on the freeway.

I called Steve, a dear friend of mine, and we put our heads together to come up with a plan on how to rescue Sean. I remembered that the adoption laws stated that, during the adoption process, Sean could not be taken out of the County without the permission of the authorities. Steve called the local Chief of Police, a friend of his, who then contacted Jack and told him that if, he did not return Sean to me, he would be arrested. Jack's parents put Sean on a plane to fly back home. Sean has never seen them or Jack since.

Now I had the energy to follow through with taking care of Sean and myself. I filed for divorce. During our divorce hearing, neither one of us had lawyers. Jack lied to the judge, telling him that I had refused to return his dead mother's belongings to him, that he was forced to drive a broken-down old car and was working nights for minimum wage. If not all lies, these were things of his doing, not something I had caused. Fortunately, he did not think to sue me for spousal support, as I believe the judge would have awarded it to him.

I was made responsible for all but the largest debt, which was the new car loan balance on the car that he had traded in for a stolen motorcycle. That debt was to be split between the two of us. I paid my half of the debt but Jack never paid on his. I was taken to small claims court, as my name was also on the initial loan documents. The judge informed me that a divorce decree did not relieve me from that obligation. I was forced to pay the remainder of the loan. Jack wound up with excellent credit, but I did not. I was furious at having to pay his part, but it was only money and now Sean and I were free from him. I was no longer a victim of domestic violence. I was wounded but not defeated.

I continued working ten-hour days, six days a week, successfully supporting Sean and me. My dear friends lived at the beach and watched Sean on Saturdays. My lawyer changed the adoption paperwork to a single parent adoption. This was so new in our county that Los Angeles County had to handle my case. I was to be the first single parent adoption applicant. Jack had refused to sign the relinquishment paperwork removing him from the adoption, so my lawyer sent him a letter demanding back child support from him. Jack then quickly signed the necessary documents, removing him all together. I was now totally free from

Jack. Never again would I be "roped" back into any kind of relationship with him.

I had been assigned a caseworker from Los Angeles. She did extensive background checks, along with interviews of my friends and co-workers. I was required to have a complete physical with chest x-rays, Pap smear and blood work. I was twenty three at the time. As I waited in the examining room for my test results, the doctor stepped outside for a cigarette break. He then came into the room and told me that I needed to quit smoking as my blood indicated the beginnings of emphysema. I had a co-worker who was suffering from severe emphysema, so I knew what he was referring to. That did not cause me to stop smoking, and luckily it had no effect on the adoption process. It was difficult having my life looked at closely. I held my breath during the whole process, as I was sure my caseworker would discover how damaged I was. It was the caseworker's job to judge if I was fit to be Sean's mother and raise him as a single parent. My blood, my lungs, my apartment, my reproductive parts, my friends, my life were all examined, documented and appraised.

At one time, my parents had assumed that they would eventually be raising Sean, as he was spending a lot of time with them before he came to live with me. They told me that they had come to the conclusion that they had screwed up with raising their four daughters, so they asked themselves if they would do anything differently with Sean. Their answer was no.

Ultimately, it was Ruth's boyfriend, Rex, who said he wanted me to raise Sean, as he loved Sean but their lifestyle was not a healthy environment for a child. Shortly after Sean came to live with me, Rex came to our apartment for a visit with Sean. It was such a sweet, heartfelt visit that I will never forget. Two months later, Rex was tragically killed in a motorcycle accident. The police officer that arrived at the scene knew Rex and held him as he died. He was the same officer that rescued me from my kidnapper. I feel deeply that Rex had come into Sean's and my life to bring us two together. We needed each other and would eventually have profound effects on each other's lives.

During the time of the adoption process, Ruth came to my house late one night. She stood in the doorway, refusing to enter. She declared that she wanted Sean back. She had just started a new relationship with an old friend and he wanted to be Sean's dad. I asked Ruth that, if she wasn't with this man, would she want Sean back and she said no. I then told her that I would never return Sean and reminded her that she had signed relinquishment papers giving me the right to have him.

The adoption process and examinations were making me a nervous wreck until I finally got up the courage to tell the caseworker that it didn't matter whether I was approved or not, Sean was staying with me and, weeks later, I received the wonderful news that I was approved. Sean was issued a new birth certificate, as my child. He was in a private school and I was working hard at learning how to be a good mother.

Through earlier neglect, Sean had been wearing shoes several sizes too small, causing his toes to overlap. To remedy this, we went to the beach every day after I got off work and walked barefoot in the sand until his toes went back to normal. On Saturday nights, we treated ourselves by putting on our pajamas, sitting on the floor in front of the television, leaning up against the hassock and eating several candy bars. We were a mini-family, beginning the healing and bonding process we so needed.

SOULTHRIVER

CHAPTER THREE

In between marriages, I had gained some weight and was now wearing size 14. While at work one day, a woman commented, with disgust, on how fat I was getting. I decided that I needed to lose weight so I stopped eating three meals a day. I was now down to 1-½ meals a day and smoking lots and lots of cigarettes. I began to obsess about my weight. I started losing weight fast, loving the results and feeling in control of my body. I also began to take lots of laxatives. I have a slightly swayed back and my stomach has a natural pooch which I detested. I wanted a concave stomach.

The more weight I lost, the more popular I became. People began asking me if I had become a vegetarian or did I have a new boyfriend. I was being rewarded for my unhealthy obsession. I became the darling at work. There were 750 employees and I was the youngest, being hired at twenty-one. This obsession with weight had caused me to become a combination of anorexic and bulimic. I felt powerful and in control. This became a very unhealthy lifestyle, a sad way to treat myself, and another form of self-punishment for being who I was. This illness had a dramatic effect on my health as I lost muscle tissue and vitality. I began to show obvious signs of having an eating disorder. Around this time, the media was featuring the deadly consequences of anorexia and bulimia. The research published showed that the common causes of those suffering from these afflictions had been tied to sexual abuse. I felt that everyone now had access to my terrible secret and I felt exposed. No longer was I proud of my extreme weight loss and I did not want to be identified as a victim of sexual abuse.

61

Times were changing and incest was no longer a taboo subject. It was being discussed in the media and people began discussing the harm it caused. I was not willing to acknowledge that I was a victim of sexual abuse. I was still in denial.

At work, I met a man who would transform my sexuality. He generously introduced me to my body. He was heaven-sent and taught me what lovemaking could truly be. He was so beautiful and kind. He awoke my natural sensuality that had been hidden and undamaged. This allowed me, for the first time, to feel sensations and desires I had never felt before. During our lovemaking I was able to achieve multiple orgasms. I had never attained orgasms before. It was truly incredible that I went from the sexual abuse from my father, then to Jack and now this. He was the angel that opened me up to allow a loving relationship into my life. He taught me how to connect with myself so that I could feel and give. He taught me to be aware of my body.

Our relationship was based on sex and the time we spent together was in my bedroom. He awakened in me a loveliness that I did not know existed. He made me feel beautiful, cherished, desirable, precious and feminine, all feelings I had never felt before. He also, unbeknownst to me, was keeping track of my periods and mentioned that I was late. I was late due to losing so much weight, not from a pregnancy. I was frightened to see that he was excited about the possibility of me being pregnant. It was then that I realized that I did not want to get pregnant, so I began taking birth control pills once again.

We had a lovely love affair and I wished it could have gone on forever but sadly I was the other woman. He was married with two children. He gave me sob stories about how bad his wife was,

62

how trapped he felt, and how he was going to leave her. I knew in my heart that I could never be his and that he could never be mine. I would never be able to trust him. Trust, for me, is one of the most important functions in a relationship. He had cheated on his wife with me and I would never be able to believe that he wouldn't do the same to me. Our wonderful love affair was short-lived but very important to my future recovery.

Six months after I ended the affair, Sean and I moved to an apartment behind my sister Jean and her boyfriend. We enjoyed spending time with them; they loved taking Sean with them on their outings, and Sean got to be with his favorite aunt. My mother worked for the School District and had summers off, so Sean spent the summers with his grandparents. Everything in my life was going well. I was repairing some of the damage and enjoying my new life.

I had a fulfilling job, good apartment and good family support. On the weekends a big group of us, sisters and friends, got together for BBQ's, drinking, dancing and having a great time. All four of us sisters, our loved ones, and friends enjoyed each other's company. It was during these fun weekends that I met Ralph, Jean's boyfriend's best friend. He was one of those nice guys I was afraid of, but decided to give him a chance. He was cute, playful, mellow, artistic and kind. He fell for me right away and had told his best friend that he was going to marry me even before we dated. He worked offshore during the week and on the weekends we saw each other at Jean's. This was a great way for me to ease into a relationship. He was sweet, young and darling. At our parties, we got to know each other better and he eventually asked me out on a date.

On our first date, we went out for dinner and dancing. That evening we went back to my apartment and made love on the living room floor. It was wonderful. I had never experienced such care and kindness during lovemaking. Afterwards, he lay naked on the floor with his head on my lap. He was open, happy and had given himself to me completely. This scared the hell out of me, but I wanted more. We quickly became a couple. Ralph worked and stayed on San Nicholas Island during the week and, on the weekends; we couldn't get enough of each other. A look, a touch would send our bodies in search of that ecstasy we shared. We stayed up until three in the morning making love, talking, touching and bonding.

Our weekends were filled with passionate lovemaking leaving me breathless. I would become flooded with emotions that I didn't understand; neither of us understood what was happening. I would become overwhelmed with tears flowing on their own. It was like being in a sun-filled desert when the calm dryness is suddenly hit with a flash flood. I did not know quite where all this was coming from, how long it would last, and what it would bring or how the devastation would leave me. In order to not feel what was brewing just below the surface, I put it off by drinking a good beer, smoking several cigarettes, smoking a little pot, doing a line of cocaine. I would be back to my numb self until the flood once again would return.

It was Ralph's love for me that broke me open. Slowly I began to connect with that injured part of me that existed due to the abuse I suffered from Jack. I had yet to access the incest memories from my childhood. I had yet to understand the connection between my feelings and some deep trauma. I kept my mind very busy and numbed out with my work, drugs, cigarettes, Sean and Ralph. I was not yet ready for the awful truth, though I was on the path to begin that journey.

When our relationship was new, we wanted to spend all our time together and would seldom leave the apartment. Sean spent most weekends with my parents. Ralph and I would be relaxing in the living room when our eyes would meet. We would go into some kind of trance and stare into each other's eyes. This lasted for sometimes up to half an hour, all the while tears rolled down our faces. I believe that we had found our soul mates and that our souls were reconnecting, healing many past wounds and preparing us for our future with experiences we would share together. When we drifted slowly out of the trance, we would return back to our reading as if nothing happened.

One warm summer morning, after making hot passionate love, Ralph looked at me and said, "We need to do something about this." I asked, "What do you mean?" He replied, "We need to get married." I agreed and four months later we were married.

Ralph continued working offshore and I continued at my job. Working at the missile plant had been great for Sean and me. I could afford to pay rent and now had medical insurance. But working six days a week, ten-hour days, was not fitting into our new lifestyle. We now lived further away and I wanted to be home on the weekends. I had no plans to quit, but it was those inconveniences that were somewhere in the back of my mind, wanting me to make a change.

My job was to coordinate assemblies, follow their activity and create reports for management. I dealt directly with the supervisors of many departments. The supervisor of the machine shop and I met on a daily basis. I was following a particularly important project through the machining process one morning and was having trouble locating it. I met with the supervisor in his office and was surprised to find the order I was looking for was there on his office floor. As I went to examine the parts, he slammed his office door shut, rushed at me, pushed himself against me, and roughly grabbed my breasts. I quickly was able to get his office door open and run out. I ran to the ladies' room and sat on the couch shivering, with fear from the assault.

A co-worker entered the bathroom, saw me in my distressed state, and asked what was wrong. When I told her what had happened, she became angry and spewed "Why did he pick you and not me?" This type of jealous reaction was the last thing I expected from her and was relieved when she left the bathroom. I sat there for several minutes, not knowing what to do next, when I heard my name over the PA system. It was announcing that the Project Manager wanted to see me in his office; he was my boss's supervisor as well as the machine shop supervisor's boss. When I arrived at the Manager's office, I found him and the machine shop supervisor waiting for me. The Manager stated that the supervisor had come to him, told him what had happened and was sorry for what he had done and the Manager asked the supervisor to leave. When we were alone, he explained to me that the "poor" supervisor's wife had a bad back, which was why he went after me and that we should feel sorry for him.

The following week, I gave my two weeks' notice. I never told Ralph about this incident as I felt that somehow, maybe, I was to blame. My mother had constantly told us girls that anything bad that happened to us was our own fault and unfortunately I still believed this sad lie. I needed to learn to take charge, fight for myself, to feel proud of my accomplishments.

On our first anniversary, we bought a mobile home in a lovely family park set behind an adult park. Sean loved living there, where he had lots of friends and he learned to swim in the park swimming pool. The place was very large and safe enough for Sean to have the freedom to ride his bike. He became known as "The Wheelie King" as he rode about the park on just his back tire. He was also very good at skateboarding and riding a motorcycle and he won races at the local BMX racing track.

I began working as the assistant manager for the family mobile home park. I was then promoted to manager of the family park and assistant manager of the adult park. I really enjoyed my work and my boss. The hardest part of the job was that, by law, I was required to have a second telephone in my house so that I was reachable by the residents 24 hours a day. Most of the calls I received concerned our antiquated water system. It was frequently breaking down and needing constant repairs. The residents would call me, furious that I hadn't given them notice that the pipes were about to break. I may have some psychic abilities but I'm not that good. Every time it rained, I received numerous calls from a gentleman reporting how disgusted he was with all the American flags that people were flying during the rain. I learned patience dealing with these calls. I was able to deal with the residents with compassion and understanding. This was a great job for me as I developed my organizational skills, learned to delegate and be assertive.

Ralph continued to work on the island for another year and, when his contract expired, he and his father purchased gardening

67

equipment and Ralph went back to his love of gardening. Ralph was kept busy with numerous clients in the park and on my days off I helped him with his various jobs. We also enjoyed spending a lot of our time together working in our own veggie/flower garden. Once again I kept very busy and life was picture perfect, in my mind. With Ralph's new vocation, we were lacking in health insurance and, in order to remedy this, I got a full-time job with the county doing accounts receivable and data entry, which I was very good at. A job requiring speed was perfect for me as I was fast and accurate. We now had family health insurance and I had vacation and sick leave with opportunities for career development and advancement. Ralph was back on the list for a government job when it became available and life was getting more adult along with its complications. We were reaching for the American dream so we did our best to look and act the part.

Several years earlier, Jean and I house-sat for our parents while they were visiting our mother's sister in Montana. When our parents went on these trips for months at a time, there was no contact with them as they did not feel it necessary to keep in touch with us. While our parents were away, our Grandma Jane received notice that the place she was renting was due to be torn down. She contacted us, saying that she needed our help in re-locating. There was no time to find her a new place, so Jean and I moved her into our parents' house. Our parents did not drink but, over the course of twenty years, had received dozens of bottles of liquor as gifts from my father's boss. In the back of our minds we may have known about all the bottles stored in their bedroom closet but didn't think anything of it, but my bloodhound Grandma found them and drank them all.

When our parents returned, they were livid at what she had done and that we had moved her into their house. They demanded that we find her a place to move into by the end of the week. Then they left again for one week while we tried to figure out what to do with Grandma. In the past, Grandma had lived in the old part of town so we starting looking there and quickly found her a place and moved her that weekend. Little did we know that we had picked the worst part of town. Luckily a distant relative of hers had a rental in a better area and, one month later, they moved her there. It was a cute little duplex where she was able to get herself a sweet little dog.

Years later, my office was within walking distance of her, allowing me to visit with her during my lunch break. She loved reading murder mysteries and the library allowed her to mark the books she had read, making it easy for me to pick out books for her. Every two weeks I went to the library checking out several books for her to read.

While I was growing up, my Grandma Jane would tell me some wild stories about our family and my mother told me it was just crazy talk. Later, when a cousin of Grandma's died, the obituary verified the truth in some of these tales. During my weekly visits, Grandma was telling me of hearing strange sounds at night, I passed them off as more of her crazy talk. She told me that her little dog had friends that came in at night and ate his food. A year earlier, she had suffered a cat scratch on her foot and refused to see a doctor about it. She had worked in hospitals for decades and had no trust in doctors. Her leg became so infected; it eventually had to be amputated. Then the other leg lost circulation and it, too, had to be removed, thus making her wheelchair bound and she started sleeping on her living room couch. The foam egg crate type mattress that my mother had bought her to keep her comfortable now needed to be turned over.

She pulled herself into her wheelchair as I lifted up the blankets, set them aside and pulled up the foam mattress. As I did, little grey flashes of fur flew around me, then out the front door, leaving behind several round warm nests of newborn baby mice tucked in between her mattress and blankets. Grandma calmly stated "Oh that must be what has been eating Pedro's food at night." I was horrified that my grandma was living this way. I knew the babies had no chance of surviving and I couldn't put the nests outside as the cats would get them, nor could they stay under Grandma. I love animals and growing up I had lots of pets; mice and rats were some of my favorites. I knew that the humane thing to do was to deal with these helpless baby mice myself. I came to the terrible conclusion that I needed to flush them down the toilet.

I remember as a child being horrified at the stories my Grandma told me of her having to put baby kittens in a gunny sack and dropping them off the end of the pier. As I was flushing helpless baby mice down the toilet, she was yelling "Baby Killer" while I was yelling "You're the crazy one living with mice in your bed." We were not mad at each other; we were mad at the situation.

As I was driving home, I was upset and embarrassed that my grandma lived like that and I hoped that no one would ever find out. When I get home, I walked through the front door to my house, relieved to be home in my safe, sane and mouse free environment. I breathed a sigh of relief and looked forward to letting that unpleasantness dissipate. I opened the back porch door

70

to our enclosed room to start a load of laundry when a mouse ran over the top of my foot. The Universe had a good laugh and I learned a large lesson of humility.

When my sister Lynn was twenty years old, she and her husband moved away to Utah. They lived all alone in the bottom of a valley, surrounded by incredible mountains and Lynn knew the name of every mountain and valley. Their cozy tiny trailer was all wood inside, was the cutest thing ever, and easy to keep warm. For income, they dug fossils, and trilobites from the earth. They had a simple and romantic life living in the vast countryside with no one else around. Lynn was not a good reader, but her husband loved to read so he introduced her to wonderful books and she soon became a prolific reader.

One Thanksgiving, my parents decided they would take their motor home to visit Lynn and her husband in Utah. My parents planned on having me, Sean, Ruth and Jean go with them. Our husbands and boyfriends were not invited. Ruth's boyfriend wanted to go as he was new to the family and wanted our parents to like him. He saw this as a good opportunity for them to get to know him better and was hurt to not be included. Ralph was pleased not to be invited as he didn't like spending time with my parents. Jean had a young son and her husband was happy to stay home with him. Ruth, Sean and I were excited about seeing Lynn again. Jean suffered from agoraphobia since early childhood and the thought of going panicked her. Ruth and I talked with her several times, trying to convince her to go but she refused. Even though we really wanted her to come with us, we respected her decision.

71

All of us girls had an unnatural fear when out doing errands, chores and shopping. I could only handle being out for a certain length of time. I was able to go to only a few places before an overwhelming cloud of anxiety and doom dropped down on top of me. I needed to get home right away stopping my shopping trips short of finishing.

Fridays were our grocery-shopping days. I would be prepared with my shopping list itemized in accordance with the store floor plan and coupons in the same order. It would cause me great distress when the store would periodically rearrange their isles. As we drove into the parking lot, anxiety would begin to creep into my arms and legs. I wanted to run, scream, and throw things. I pounded on the steering wheel. I did not want to enter the store. There was no reasoning with me or with myself about what was going on. We would sit in the parking lot until I got the nerve to get out of the car and do the "fucking shopping." I always started in the same place in the store. I would grab a cart, grip my list in hand and set off to do my weekly shopping. I was barely communicable. If I returned to our cart with an item in my hand and found that Ralph had already put the same item in the cart, I would feel my body fill with rage as I threw the duplicate item back onto the shelf.

When I approached a shelf with a coupon for an item and that item had several brands or contained several of the same items, I could not focus. I became overwhelmed, my senses went haywire, my vision began to distort and the shelf would grow, fall back away from me or fall towards me. I would freeze in panic until Ralph would find me and help me with my selection. Once we were able to get the items we needed I would push the cart to the checkout line. I would breathe a sigh of relief that once again I had made it. But as I stood in line I would began to hyperventilate. On two occasions I actually passed out in line; both times, I was alone and depended on strangers to help me.

My sister Jean had the same experiences. She lived one block from her grocery store and shopped every day for the few things she needed. Her therapist connected her agoraphobia to our father. When we went shopping with our father, it was always torture. He must have had anxiety around shopping as well. People frequently commented on my long gait and fast stride, which came from me trying as hard as I could to keep up with him as he hit the ground running from car to counter. As a union man, he would only buy things made in America and would only shop at Sears so, by God, they better have what he needed. The minute he opened the car door, he was angry. He was angry at the things being made in China, angry that he felt limited to what and where he could shop, angry at what this country was coming to. He walked as fast as he could while the four of us trailed behind for, if we didn't keep up, we knew we would be left behind.

When he was done at the checkout counter, he would turn around, slap the backs of our heads as our signal that he was done and that we were returning to the car. We were convinced that he would not look for us or even wait for us to catch up with him. We felt certain he would drive away. Our focus was entirely on keeping him in our sights. I agree with Jean's therapist, who told her that it is no wonder we have panic attacks when out and about.

Ruth and I totally understood Jean's decision to stay home and not travel with us to Utah, though we really did want her to go with us. It had been a couple of years since the four of us had been together and we selfishly wanted her to help buffer the negative energy from our parents. Jean had a baby and husband at home and we understood. Our father was furious that he was unable to force us all to do what he wanted. Both our parents hounded Jean for weeks before we were to leave. On the day of the trip, they drove to Jean's house and demanded that she get in the motor home. I have to give her a lot of credit for taking care of herself and saying no to my father. I don't think I could have done it......back then.

There we all were: Sean, Ruth, my parents and I, along with the turkey dinner all packed in the motor home, headed towards Utah. On the way, my father announced that we were parking overnight in Las Vegas and we would all be watching a kiddie show. This sounded intriguing, I had never liked the idea of the adult shows, but the kiddie show should be fun to watch. The price was $25 which was a lot of money for Ruth and me. The trip was beginning to affect us. We were reverting back to being children. We were in close quarters under the direct influence of our parents, and we felt that we had no options.

Sean was eleven at the time and excited to be in Las Vegas. We joined the line to buy our tickets. Whilst in line, my father told us he had to go to the men's room and motioned to Sean to follow him. Sean told his grandfather that he didn't have to go and his grandfather pulled back his fist and punched him directly in the chest and yelled "NOW!"

I was stunned as I watched them march off to the restroom. I was livid. I was still in that little girl space and demanded that my mother do *something*, *anything*, say *something* to my father. She told me to do it myself. I was feeling tormented by this

74

predicament. At first I was angry that my mother wouldn't fix this for me and I felt my body start to react to the situation. I realized that I needed to grow up and take care of Sean. I needed to do the right thing. There was no way I would allow myself to stuff this, to ignore what had just happened. On the trip, energy has been building up as Ruth and I listened to the stories our parents were telling as we drove across country. Their version was alien to us. Their stories always showed them as our heroes, protectors, defenders, always doing the right thing for their daughters, and we knew better. We remembered the events like it was yesterday and it was making me sick. I had enough and I needed to act.

When Sean and my father returned, I told my father that it was wrong for him to hit Sean. He dismissed my complaint and said that Sean knew what was going on. I hated being there. I felt trapped in my childhood once again. I was feeling a loss of control and fearful for my son.

We were seated in a crowd of families when a comedian came out on stage and started telling adult jokes about boobs and sucking boobs. Sean soon forgets about the punch in the chest and enjoyed the jokes. The jokes were making me uncomfortable. When the comedian finished with his skit I was relieved and ready for the kiddie show to begin. The show began, it was a replica of the movie Splash, and all the showgirls were bare-breasted. My father and Sean were getting really excited. I was disgusted. Once again I felt that I was a partner in my father's sexual pleasures. This was inappropriate for my son and not appropriate for a father/daughter activity.

Due to the incest, I was very uncomfortable around sexuality and this situation was making my insides feel both anxious and furious. I had paid to see this and my father demanded that I stay. I was consumed with fear and disgust. I felt like a voyeur in collaboration with my father. Would this relationship never change?

We did have a wonderful visit with Ruth and the trip home was uneventful and it helped me to see what our family dynamics were like and how uncomfortable they made me feel.

Most of my coping skills were not healthy, but I needed them to stay alive. At sixteen I started to smoke cigarettes, curing me of my nail-biting. In my mind, nail- biting was an awful habit that I could not hide, which further added to my shame. I felt as though my chewed up fingernails gave evidence to the fact that I was not psychologically well. My father was a chronic nail-bitter, though I cannot recall ever seeing him bite his fingernails.

Cigarettes became by best friend and were socially acceptable. They were calming, soothing and relaxing just like the commercials said. I started smoking to look cool and soon realized that it helped me with my anxiety. By the time I was thirty years old I was smoking two packs a day. Amphetamines became my other best friend. Due to the abuse, I was hyper and hyper-vigilant. The amphetamines kept me energized and the cigarettes kept my anxiety at a tolerable level. I liked being hyper as it kept me busy, alert and aware of my surroundings, giving me the sense that I could protect myself. During this period, I had a super-clean house, was doing great at work and had a beautifully manicured garden, and I was working myself to exhaustion. I kept constantly busy and was not able to go to bed until the house was completely tidied up, though I still was not able to sleep the night through.

On cleaning day, I would kick Sean and Ralph out of the house and I would become a cleaning madwoman. I would clean as fast as I could with muscles tense and back rigid as I raced through the house. The vacuum cleaner took the brunt of my anger as I flung it from room to room dinging walls as I went. My mother told me that, when I was a baby and would cry, she would turn on the vacuum cleaner so she wouldn't have to hear me. In talking with my sisters, they told me they also have a dislike for their vacuum cleaner. So Mr. Vacuum was my enemy, my evil dance partner. I flung him from room to room, the canister flying behind me banging into walls and furniture, beating the crap out of everything. I went through a lot of vacuum cleaners. When Ralph and Sean would return, they would find a clean house and an exhausted housewife.

Once I discovered cocaine, I was in an altered state of heaven. I quickly become addicted. While I was in the hospital for surgery, I was on a post-surgery morphine drip. I had taken cocaine with me to the hospital, safely tucked away in my cigarette packet. I was snorting cocaine as morphine dripped into my veins, all the while continuously smoking cigarettes. I am surprised I didn't kill myself with the speedball combination or catch my bed on fire in my drugged-up state.

Ralph and I both were heavy cigarette smokers, I had been taking birth control pills for thirteen years, and I was smoking up to two packs of cigarettes a day. Back then, we were allowed to smoke at work and, as my fingers flew on the keyboard, every ten seconds or so I reached for a deep soothing drag. New health studies were being published that it was dangerous to be smoking while taking birth control pills and, since we didn't want any more children, Ralph suggested we quit smoking. He had no problem quitting. I, on the other hand, was another story. I took a free smoking cessation course at the Seventh Day Adventist Church which was very informative and supportive, but I couldn't quit. I lied to Ralph, making him think I had, but I hadn't. I had not spent a day without my "best friend" in my lungs; I was extremely addicted. About that time, a study came out announcing that quitting smoking was more difficult than quitting heroin.

I had what we affectionately called lung cheese. While laughing, coughing or even during a lively conversation, a disgusting looking, hideously smelling, chunk of what looked like cheese would unexpectedly fly out of my mouth. I could also do a neat parlor trick where I would pound on my chest (no cigarettes involved) and blow smoke out of my mouth. I knew health-wise I needed to quit, so I took on this task as I would tackle any challenge. I am a strong-willed, redheaded, blue-eyed lefty that can do just about anything I put my mind to, but I couldn't do this. I snuck a cigarette whenever possible.

One of my passions was my morning jog ending, with a cigarette. I was consumed with nicotine twenty-four hours a day and would awake several times a night to have a smoke. My anxiety level would go through the roof whenever I went an hour without my nicotine fix as I tried to stave off lighting up as long as I could. First the anxiety would kick in and then the rage. This was a physical rage. My body would go into a fury. I could not reason with this addictive demand that had me feeling as if I wanted to kill.

For another year, I continued this battle, losing to the amount of up to one pack a day. Ralph had returned to working on the island so, during the week, I only needed to hide my smoking from Sean. I blamed my co-workers for the smoke smell on me and I used every excuse to be alone to smoke. I frequently went for long walks, to the store, collect the mail, anything I could think of to be by myself with my best friend, tobacco. Sean was always asking to go with me and I continuously said no. I was a desperate all- consumed smoker.

When I ran out of cigarettes, I resorted to digging in ash trays, any ashtray I could find. The best resource was the tall ash cans outside of stores, they held the longest butts. When they were empty, I resorted to looking in the ditches for butts, cigarettes or cigars, it didn't matter. I don't know what I thought about all this or what people I knew thought when they saw me doing this. All I cared about was finding my next cigarette fix. I was wearing out my welcome with my friends and neighbors as I was constantly bumming cigarettes from them. All my thoughts were on where I could get my next cigarette. During times of rational thought, probably just after I finished a cigarette, I pondered why I couldn't stop this terrible habit. I didn't want to live like this. I didn't want to be consumed with this deadly habit. Why was I allowing cigarettes to control my life and health? I had no idea why. If this was harder to quit than heroin, then I was worse off than a heroin addict and I acted like one

On my thirtieth birthday, we bought a cute little cottage; it was built in 1928. It had a large greenhouse in the back with decks and later Ralph built a fishpond. We grew our own veggies and flowers and our money went into fixing up the house. We were living the American dream.

Then Ralph found cigarettes in my purse. I used the excuse that my dear friend at work, who was like a mother to me, had just found out that her breast cancer had returned after being clear for five years. I told him that is why I started smoking and he was a bit sympathetic. This was low of me. I was lying. I finally had to admit to him that I had never stopped. He then told me that he would rather I cheat on him than smoke cigarettes. The following day, I made an appointment with our doctor to see if he could help me.

At my appointment, I told the doctor what Ralph had said and the doctor understood the significance of my emergency visit. He prescribed a brand new medicine that was to help people quit smoking; it was called Nicorette gum, my newest best friend. The idea was that it supplied nicotine to my system to help with the cravings and the physical response that caused me to reach for a cigarette. I was to place the gum in my mouth, where it was to rest between my check and gums, bite down on it a couple of times when I felt a craving. That is what I was supposed to do; that is not what I did. I chewed it like it was the best tasting gum in the world. I slept with it in my mouth, waking up several times a night to chew on it some more. I broke nearly every filling in my mouth, but no cigarette touched my lips.

The information on this medication was that it was to be used only for a three-month-long period. I knew this, so instead of checking back with my doctor, I kept going directly to the pharmacy to get the prescription refilled. The gum was really working for me, nicotine was flowing through my veins and was my new "girlfriend" and we were as happy as can be. I no longer smelled like smoke, the gum was paid for through my insurance, no more sneaking around, no more digging for butts and no need to purchase cigarettes. This was great! I could live like this forever. I chewed Nicorette gum non-stop for six months. I went to the local pharmacy, where everyone working there knew me by name, to get my refills. The pharmacy was packed with people as I strolled up and placed my order. I stood back with the crowd awaiting my delicious gum. The pharmacist yelled out to me "Sarah, the doctor says that, since you haven't cut back at all you can't have any more." Oh my god, I was devastated. Not only could I not get my refill, the other customers didn't know what it was I had not cut back. I imagined the people looking down and shaking their heads because I was a drug addict who wasn't being good. And dammit I am not a drug addict; I just needed help quitting smoking. Cigarettes aren't a drug, at least that is what I told myself.

I was humiliated and dragged my sorry butt home. For the last six months, I had in my purse three cigarettes, just in case of an emergency. They were sorry looking, stinky, crushed up sticks of tobacco, but I did not touch them!!! I carried those same three cigarettes for five years, never smoking them. I physically no longer craved cigarettes and found to my surprise that I could cope without the gum. My nicotine addiction had been cured.

SOULTHRIVER

CHAPTER FOUR

Then the horrible nightmare began. I started to experience bouts of depression and rage. I would awaken at night and eat four or five cookies, as they became my cigarette substitute. They say you should use carrots as cigarettes but that didn't work for me. I began to be unable to handle conflict without going into a rage. My brain was not processing information correctly. I was raw, vulnerable, and out of control. My hyper vigilance was no longer working. I was unable to keep the enemy away as I became my enemy when my coping skills no longer worked. Keeping the house spotless, working myself to exhaustion, being prepared for anything, all these seemed foreign to me now.

I shut down. I stopped talking. Talking took so much effort. When smoking, each exhale relaxed me, gave me a sense of peace, and now every exhale was exhausting. I spent time not breathing. It became too laborious to be alive. I was reprimanded at work because I had stopped communicating with my co-workers. I went from hyper-chatty, chain-smoking Sarah to an inactive lump. I was a mess. Once nicotine was no longer a constant companion, everything changed. Worst of all, my sex life changed.

Without cigarettes, the craziness intensified as I was either experiencing depression or rage. I couldn't find a physical replacement. During my smoking era, I was up at 4 am, for my morning jog, seldom ever sat still, always moving. Looking back, I wonder if I would have done better with some form of medication, but my therapist never did recommend any. I am not certain that doctors were aware of the day-to-day, minute-to-minute effects cigarettes have on the human body. The obsession created by the body's constant demand for nicotine made life hell and cigarettes provided relief. I am very cautious about recommending to anyone to stop smoking without a strong support system. I couldn't sleep through the night without the body cravings waking me up.

I no longer had cigarettes to calm me down or to bring me to the present or make me feel safe. I began to have what is called night terrors. In the dark of the night, the world would change into a very scary place. I would revert to that helpless little girl who frantically tried to keep her pajamas on. The thousands of voices in my head began yelling, commanding, denigrating and terrorizing me, causing my body to be racked with anxiety. I was hyperventilating, unable to relax, calm down, read or write. My body took over as my mind went crazy. I was like a child in the middle of a temper tantrum, unable to remember why I was so upset and unable to take care of myself.

I was inconsolable and aware that I didn't want to wake Ralph and Sean from their peaceful slumber. I didn't want them to see me this way. I dreaded the loving concern, the caring questions "What do you need?" and "What can I do for you?" and the confusing question of "Sarah, what is wrong?" I had no idea what was causing this, nor how to stop it; I could not explain it. When not in a rage or filled with anxiety, I was bedridden with depression. I don't recall how long this went on before I started to remember about the abuse.

More and more memories flooded my mind, making me feel more and more crazy. I couldn't do this on my own any longer. This secret was consuming, devouring, and controlling me. It made so much sense now why I was so highly addicted to tobacco. The tobacco kept these feelings down, numbed me and caused me to focus on my next cigarette. Now without tobacco and finding nothing to replace it, I was a complete mess and I needed Ralph to know what was happening to me. I needed professional help. I knew once I told him, everything would change with us. I dreaded the thought of having to tell him. Would he think I was an awful person, dirty, tainted, and evil? Would he confront my parents with this, which I could not handle at this point in my life? Would he still love me? All was unknown to me as to how he would react.

We were having dinner at his parents' house when I became overwhelmed and needed to tell him my horrible secret. After dinner, he and I went for a walk to the river bottom. There were eucalyptus trees illuminated by the setting sun, allowing filtered sunshine to brighten our path. Delicate flowers were at our feet, a very pretty scene for a tragic unveiling. We sat down and, as I began to tell him, I was consumed with nerves and anxiety. I flung my arms around, walked away, walked back, and walked away again. This was so difficult. I started to panic and that started to scare Ralph. He realized that I had something to tell him yet he had no idea what was troubling me. Finally I forced myself to blurt out that I had been molested by my father, from the age of four, until I married and moved away at the age of seventeen. Ralph's first words after hugging me were, "That explains a lot, things make more sense now." We agreed that I needed professional help. I felt such relief at his reaction. By revealing my secret, I was admitting that the abuse was real. I was filled with hopefulness, knowing that there are professionals in this world that could help me.

When I did see my doctor to get a referral, required by my insurance, he cried that I had reached out to him, and because of what had happened to me. He recommended a therapist who was familiar with helping people with childhood abuse and trauma. By opening up that part of my life that had been torn from me and placed in the ceiling a long time ago allowed me to turn in the direction of the agonizing path of my recovery.

Every minute, I was shaken with how my life was changing. This was scary, hard shit. My whole body would react with anger. Overwhelming emotions caused my vision to leave and all I could see was black. I would curl up in a ball and hide, sometimes in the bathroom, or the closet, or a corner of the house. As horrible as this process was becoming, the more determined I became that I was never going to go back to the way things had been before. That would be worse than what I was experiencing now. I wanted to live. I wanted to feel normal, happy, joyful, sensuous, alive and clean. The psychologist that my doctor referred me to was a kind, patient, understanding and professional man. I wasn't sure about working these deep personal issues with a man, but I think at this point I trusted men more than I did women. I felt that women would betray me, set me up for failure, and lure me to dark passages. I realized I felt this way due to my relationship with my mother. I felt that she sacrificed me to my father and had evil feelings for me. I believed that my father had evil designs towards me but didn't feel evilness towards me. I was made to feel that I ruined my mother's life, not so with my father. I know that victims tend to identify with their abuser and that their anger is usually directed towards the other parent, normally the mother. I know that this three-sided relationship is very unhealthy and that I have some crazy beliefs and feelings surrounding this family dynamic. I was just barely sticking a tip of my finger out of the shit pile. I was breathing, eating and functioning with the weight of the shit of my childhood and hopefully this doctor could help me climb out of this hell. I struggled to free myself from this intense pull on me as the suction became stronger and stronger, trying to pull me back in.

SOULTHRIVER

CHAPTER FIVE

The county that I worked for began offering self-improvement classes, leadership training, assertiveness training, and group dynamics training. I signed up for everything. At the first class I attended, we were required to fill out a personality questionnaire. I thought that I filled the forms out just like they wanted; my truth seemed okay to me and I was excited to see my results. When my results came back, I was told they were pretty bad, showing that I was lacking in self-esteem. I was in such denial. What in my belief system was lacking self-esteem? I was embarrassed and ashamed. The only thing that saved me was that coincidently I had recently started therapy, just as the results had suggested.

My mother had decided she would like to have her handwriting analyzed and she paid for herself and the four of us girls to have it done. There was a form we each filled out with our information. I was nervous doing this, as I didn't know what my handwriting would reveal. A month later, the results arrived at my mother's house. She asked us all to come read our results. When we arrived, we discovered that she had already read her results and chose not to share them with us. Being the oldest, I read mine first. I was so apprehensive yet also excited to hear what it had to say about me and maybe learn about my future potentials and talents. I read it aloud. The report talked about the abusive childhood I had experienced, my lack of self-esteem, and that I needed to seek professional help to deal with and recover from my past.

There it was in black and white, straight from my own fingers. I felt that the truth about me was finally being revealed to my mother and that I would be punished. I imagined her saying what a bad child I was, complaining through my fingertips about my childhood and how dare I talk about my parents in such a way? But instead she said "Well, mine said the same thing," and we went to the next daughter's results. I don't remember what theirs said. I became numb, my hearing and sight closed in on me. Here was the woman that raised me, dismissing my childhood experience that she had co-created with my father and I felt no empathy from her. As with all ugly things in my childhood, we did not speak about it again. That pink elephant in the living room was just getting bigger and bigger. I was suffocating from the unspoken. I was choking on my own internal screams. And yet I now realize that this was yet another way the Universe was trying to communicate to me that my family had been, and still was, very toxic to my very being and enmeshed in the very essence of who I was.

Once I told Ralph about my father, I could not un-ring that bell. My sister Jean was married to Ralph's best friend and we were friends with my other sisters' boyfriends. Ralph felt obligated to warn them about my father. Jean's husband told Ralph that he had no personal problem with my father and the other two said nothing. Jean had a son and daughter and we were worried about the children's safety. Jean was spending a lot of time with my parents, so I felt compelled to explain to my little niece that my father, her grandpa, had done bad things to me when I was a little girl, that he touched my private parts and made me touch his. Amazingly, she stood up tall, puffed up her chest and loudly exclaimed that her dad had never done anything like that to her. I was so glad to hear this and I explained to her that I was talking about her grandpa and to please tell me or someone else if her grandpa ever did anything like that to her. I later found out that Jean never left her children alone with my parents.

Therapy for me was a very, very difficult process. In the beginning, I found myself feeling ill on Mondays, the day of my appointment. I frequently wanted to cancel my session, but my therapist pointed out why I felt sick on Mondays, so I made the effort to be there, and be on time. I can't stress enough that therapy is hard work. The emotional trauma I was dealing with was affecting me physically. I had high cholesterol, aches and pains in my arms and legs, headaches, neck aches, even my toes hurt. Every time I went to the doctor, I would remind him that I was in therapy and asked him if my current problem could be caused by stress. Every time he said yes. As bad as it got, I never wanted to go back to my previous life. I was on my path to recovery. It was ugly, painful and emotional but I desperately wanted to get better. At the end of some of the most difficult sessions, my therapist would ask if I wanted Ralph to come pick me up and I always said no. Getting to my appointment was more difficult. Sometimes I would go into a rage as I left home to drive to my appointment. Ralph would call the therapist's office to make sure I got there safely.

A big part of my therapy involved me telling my story and being heard and my therapist and I would discuss what I had revealed. He would guide me to reach out to that time and place, feel the feelings that my inner child had so repressed. Most of these feelings were never initially experienced. A child would implode with the enormity of what was happening to her, who was doing it and that it would happen repeatedly over and over. These experiences with my father may have only taken twenty minutes, but I spent the rest of the day and night trying to push down the experience and escape my reality. I have read that the abuse I suffered changed my very DNA, that my body holds all the memories, emotions and pain I had experienced. My job now was to heal from that trauma.

It was so shaming, ugly and painful to admit that these things happened to me. My crazy thoughts would tell me that I must have done something to deserve this. I wasn't a good enough daughter, deserving a father who would cherish and protect me. My belief system also told me that I didn't deserve a mother who would keep me from harm, who would love me and think I was wonderful. I thought I must have asked for this because I thought an adult wouldn't do these things to a good loveable child. I was now telling all of this to a total stranger. Once I admitted the truth about myself, I didn't know how I would be able to live in the world, be a wife, a mother, an employee, a neighbor or a friend. I needed therapy to keep me alive and help me stay alive.

My therapist recommended a book on incest that could help me develop coping skills. The book would be able to provide me with the information that I needed to help me get through the remaining six days of the week. I went to the large local library but they had nothing available on their shelves. I then went to the small bookstore downtown and found that they, too, had nothing on their shelves about incest. I was getting desperate and frustrated. I gathered up my courage and asked the bookstore owner if he would order the book for me. I was embarrassed to have to say the title out loud but I was determined to learn what I could. If my therapist recommended something, I was going to do it. Two weeks later, I got the phone call that my book was in. I ran down to the bookstore, paid for my book and clutched it to my chest, tears streaming down my face. Just knowing that someone would write a book about my abuse was encouraging.

The author outlined the effects of sexual abuse and recommended ways to heal. This felt like a timely gift from the heavens. I learned that what had happened to me was not only bad, it was against the law. I was so encouraged to learn that adults had taken the time, money and determination to create laws against these heinous acts. I became thirsty for knowledge as I immersed myself in the subject matter concerning childhood sexual abuse. The more I wanted to know, the more the Universe showed me. Unfortunately, I became obsessed and over-exposed myself which was re-traumatizing me, a common dilemma with victims. This obsession began to take me away from looking at my issues and placing my focus square in the middle of the world's problems. I saw incest every time I saw a father with his young daughter. Incest became a dark cloud coloring everything I saw and filled my head with these thoughts. I became a vigilante. I was hyper-alert and hyper-vigilant. I was placing myself back into the victim role. I became a self-righteous, self-appointed spokesperson and watchdog. These were all ways for me to get immersed with the problem and take the focus off of myself

I decided that my sisters needed the benefit of my newly acquired knowledge. I felt the need to educate them on their childhood and the effects it was having on their current lives. I felt that I needed to tell them why we were all so fucked up. I overwhelmed them with the knowledge of our childhood. I reminded them of the awful things we all had experienced. They were not prepared to hear what I had to say. I alienated them with my repeated insistence. I was determined to break down their walls of protected denial. I was ready to heal them, save them. I was ready to be everything for them. I was focusing on them instead of myself. I wanted them on my side. When I told them of the sexual abuse I suffered from our father, my two youngest sisters did not believe me.

Ruth finally told them that what I was saying was true, that she had seen our father come into our bedroom at night and make me take off my pajamas while he fondled me. I felt the room break apart as we all had our own shift in consciousness and reality. Then we once again pushed everything down and went back to preparing for that evening's party. I was spending time trying to heal others without first healing myself. This was yet another way for me to escape looking into the torment that followed me around. I needed to face my inner demons and save my inner child.

I was beginning to allow myself to feel old feelings. It was a very important part of the healing process to identify the abuse, to recognize what I felt as a child, sympathize with that child and begin the healing process. What I needed to do was focus on myself and not the whole world. I could be of no help to anyone else until I helped myself.

One therapy group that I was in was facilitated by a male therapist and a woman who was a well-known spiritual advisor. We were asked to do lots of journaling, collages, and picture boards surrounding our abuse. One such project was to document certain parts of our lives. We were, if possible, to take pictures of where we grew up. At that time, I lived within minutes of two of the houses I grew up in. I first visited the house where the sexual abuse began. Being there was so physically difficult for me that I began breathing rapidly and I was sweating and shaking as I stood in the street in front of the house. I could not go into the yard, let alone into the house. I was frozen with fear and dread. I was unable to get the camera to work. I could not take pictures for my workbook. This was my proof of how devastating the effect of the abuse was still having on me. I hated not being able to finish this project. I was frozen by what had happened to me thirty-two years earlier. I was experiencing PTSD (Post Traumatic Stress Disorder), normally associated with war veterans. I realized that I would not let this ruin my life; I wanted to live. I wanted to be a good wife, good mother, and good neighbor. I realized that there was no healing in running from myself. It had been decades since I suffered the abuse and the effects were not going to go away on their own. No matter how good I looked on the outside, my insides needed healing.

One of my first physical healings came through my own intuition. I was working a forty-minute commute from home. One day on my drive to work, I noticed that my face was in a perpetual smile, much like a clown's mask. I told myself that it looked artificial and that all I needed to do was just relax my face. I took a deep breath and tried to create a calm, relaxed-looking expression. As I relaxed I felt pain in my facial muscles. The pain was unreal. My facial muscles complained as if I had been sitting in the dentist chair for hours with my mouth wide open. My intuition told me that this was a very important goal for me to achieve. I practiced for a few seconds working up to minutes of relaxed expression. I did this every morning and evening on my drives to and from work. At the end of two weeks, a relaxed face became my normal expression. As my face relaxed, the rest of my body began to also relax. This also helped with the jaw injury I had suffered years ago.

I feel fortunate that, at the age of thirty, I started my path to recovery. It felt as if the world surrounding me was providing me with many opportunities. I attended healing workshops and the community college offered several classes in personal healing. John Bradshaw was on television and Robert Bly was doing retreats in our town. ACA (Adult Children of Alcoholics) had meetings nearly every night. My healing and survival process became my priority. I dove into these functions heart first. The "New Age," "Airy Fairy," "Touchy Feely," "Inner Child," "Rebirthing," "Dream Work" and "Primal Scream" movements became my focus. I was absorbing the love and information through my heart and skin. I now had friends who had similar experiences and issues and we joined together to create a "family of choice." I listened to men tell their stories and I started to care about them. I was swimming in the healing river of love and compassion. Every weekend was dedicated to this process. Ralph and I both immersed ourselves in these wonderful experiences that filled us with joy. Life became more than just working to pay our bills. We now had moments (sometimes only seconds) in our lives where we felt true peace and love.

I was working full time and going to night school to improve my employment potential. I was seeing my therapist once a week. Sean was spending the weekends with my parents. This was great for Ralph and me during our honeymoon period. It allowed us to bond, create dreams, plan for our future and enjoy each other as fully as possible. But the week was so different from our weekends. The week was a struggle for our newly created family. Most of our time with Sean was spent correcting his homework, taking him to his soccer practice, and monitoring his chores, all the while struggling to create a loving household within our instant family. The week involved correcting, directing, cleaning, educating, activities we needed to do for Sean. At the end of one particularly difficult week, we were relieved that we would have a break from Sean as well as he from us. Ralph then realized that our recreational fun weekend time was not being spent as a family and that we needed to spend more time with our son. My parents had dictated to us their demands and expectations when it came to Sean spending time with them. When Ralph broached the idea that we confront them, I believed that possibly they would get mad at me. Ralph reassured me that they wouldn't mind and that it was a reasonable request, as we would be sharing our time with Sean. Sean could spend every other weekend with his grandparents and this sounded very reasonable to me, a great compromise and should make everyone happy.

I excitedly called my father with this great idea. He blew up, demanding to know what we would be doing with Sean on "our" weekends. I couldn't believe that this was happening. In my mind, this was such a great way to function as a loving family. Slowly my father calmed down. I'm not clear as to what calmed him down, maybe my mother, maybe something I said, maybe out of respect for Ralph or just maybe because in two days it was their weekend with Sean. I don't know, but he calmed down until the next weekend when it was our "turn" to have Sean with us. Saturday morning at 6 am the phone rang, jolting us out of bed. It was my father demanding to know why we were still in bed and what did we have planned for our weekend with Sean. He succeeded in thoroughly shaking me up. I was a wreck; once again I was a four-year-old little girl terrified of displeasing my father. When I began telling my father what we had planned, he slammed the phone down in my ear.

This was a rude awakening that maybe something was wrong with my family dynamic, the role I played, and the unhealthy effect this might be having on my life. The rose colored glasses started to lose their masking effect and I was quite shocked at what I was seeing, experiencing and feeling. A simple request to spend every other weekend with our own son became the undoing of my father's tight, suffocating, incestuous grip on me. I began to try to deal with the physical aspects of his controlling methods as I created physical barriers to protect our family. I wasn't even close to being able to deal with the emotional ensnarement and entanglements that kept me so tied to them. To tame this internal battle would take many, many years of therapy and growth.

I was in an emotional state that began affecting my sleep. If I was asleep and Ralph happened to touch me in any way, my body would fling itself upright, wide awake and ready to flee. It was a terrifying feeling that shook me to my core. I was in denial at that time of why I was suddenly repulsed and fearful. We both began to dread the accidental touch that might happen during the night and were happy that we had a king-sized bed.

During lovemaking, Ralph's face began to turn into my father's face and I would be re-traumatized all over again. Here I was an adult in my own home with my loving husband and I was being invaded by the trauma of my incest. I was repulsed, fearful and anxious around lovemaking. Our relationship had started out like a fairy tale love story and now it was a horror movie. It was very important for my recovery that I reclaim the natural and beautiful sexual acts that we are all meant to enjoy. I was determined to not allow my father and ex-husband to rob me of this. I was now married to a wonderful and kind man and wanted to create an intimacy that I had never experienced before.

I told my therapist of my wanting to achieve a healthy and loving intimacy with my husband. He recommended a self-help book for incest victims that described ways to recover healthy sexuality. The book told me how to create a safe setting with rules and thankfully Ralph agreed to the rules as we slowly worked on healing this very important part of our relationship.

Ralph agreed that I could stop our lovemaking at any time I needed to without any repercussions from him. We started with eliminating any smells, such as motor oil and certain colognes that would trigger me, reminding me of my father or Jack. In the beginning, my breasts were off limits, as touching them made me angry and jittery. During sex, I was to keep my eyes open and focused on Ralph's face at all times. The minute that his face changed to my father's or Jack's, we stopped what we were doing. It was a very scary challenge. We never knew when the transference would take place and it was always on our minds. What would start out as a dance of love with my beloved would sometimes end with me curled up in a ball, drenched in my own tears. Sex was re-triggering me and I would become racked with guilt, disgust and despair. This was not a challenge for the weak. This was fucking hard work, but we stuck to it. I was determined to make this work. I loved Ralph and our relationship came first. As scary as it was, I wanted this part of me healed. I refused to be robbed of such a wonderful aspect of being a human being.

Ralph and I continued with working on recovering my sexuality. The rules, along with the precautions that we had agreed to, seemed to start working. Slowly I was able to stay in the room a little longer with fewer and fewer setbacks as the transferences happened less and less.

Life was evolving as we continued on our path to recovery. We stopped joining my family for weekend parties. Ralph had stopped drinking and we both had stopped smoking pot and snorting cocaine. We began to fill our free time with activities focused on healing our inner demons and we spent more time playing with Sean. I began taking classes at the Community College that centered on healing the inner child. A dream class had a dynamic teacher who focused on childhood sexual abuse. I learned how to interpret my dreams and I was able to listen to other students' dreams as the teacher helped us to understand their meanings. From that class, the teacher began a therapy group in his house.

The group was made up of men and women, ages ranging from thirty to seventy. It was in this group where I met wonderful wounded men and women who were willing to tell their stories. We met once a week in the evenings for two to three hours. We each checked in as to how our week went and how we were doing. In our check-in, we needed to include three things we had accomplished that week as well as how we felt. This was very helpful and important for our growth to be able to recognize positive things happening in our lives that we were creating during this difficult period of healing. We also learned to recognize and understand our feelings. Most of us had shut down our feelings and replaced them with reactions. When we could identify how we were feeling, then we could search out what the causes of those feelings were in order to deal with them. We witnessed each other's current struggles and stories stemming from our past as we learned to give helpful feedback to each other. In these men, I recognized their inner child as weak, vulnerable and innocent as I was. This was extremely helpful for me, as I had previously seen all men as only perpetrators. I did not trust any man around any young girls. It would cause me panic attacks when I saw a man alone with a young girl, be it in a park, taking a walk or in a car. Triggering me, I would feel "regressed" as if I was in danger, and I was intensely fearful for the young girl. It felt like I needed to rescue her. I often wanted to run up to them, grab the girl and run. It was very hard to stop myself from doing so. Of course, it was my own inner child that needed the rescuing. I needed to focus on my own experiences within myself. Now I was learning how to do this in the therapy group. In group, I could vocalize and act out my gut reaction and then I would receive helpful, honest feedback. This was great practice for how I wanted to function in the world. I was beginning to build coping tools to use that enabled me to react the way I wanted to.

After three years of participating in my first therapy group, the therapist chose another member, my friend Peter, and me to be his sidekicks. When someone didn't know the answer to a question or answered the question incorrectly, the therapist would call on either Peter or me to answer, which we proudly did. I was falling back into the trap of focusing on other people's recovery instead of my own. I monitored others, judging their progress. I realized that it was not in my best interest, nor could I afford the time, to be focusing on someone else's recovery only to make me feel better, superior or smarter. I, too, would have challenges and bottoms to hit, with deep holes to pull myself out of, as I continued on my path to recovery.

Therapy tends to have its highs and lows and I was in the high functioning period. This allowed me time to breathe, clear up any recent wreckage, and take care of the maintenance of myself. My self-esteem was at an all-time high, making this the perfect time for me to get a physical, get my teeth cleaned, apply for a new job/position, and go on a vacation. All of these were rewards to me for doing this hard work. I was successfully dragging myself to therapy every week, reading my recovery books, doing my collages, going to work, while on some days just barely getting out of bed. The world was becoming a brighter, fuller, and happier place for me. Colors became more intense, vibrant, and illuminating.

I made great friends in my first therapy group. We spent a lot of time together doing exciting and new things. We helped each other out with our interactions within the outside world. Together we took workshops, went to spiritual activities, and we played. We all started attending ACA (Adult Children of Alcoholics) 12-step meetings. These meeting brought me back to myself, back to focusing on my own recovery. Unlike group therapy, there was no cross talk or feedback allowed in these meetings. I was no longer able to show off or be the teacher's pet. I no longer dwelled in my mind but in my heart. I witnessed peoples' stories in group therapy, enabling me to be able to listen to what others shared. Within the walls of these meetings, I felt very safe. I began to learn new ways to have friends, relax, to have compassion, and reach out for help. The 12-step meetings provided literature and I read everything I could get my hands on. There were workbooks designed to address almost everything I was willing to admit. I was not a child of alcoholics but my parents were raised by alcoholics; therefore, I am a grandchild of alcoholics which has its own set of unique problems and challenges. There also are wonderful books that address this family dynamic.

We girls couldn't gauge our parents' emotional state based on how many empty bottles were in the house or run when we heard the sound of a beer bottle opening. Our parents were always totally unpredictable; they "white knuckled it" through life, swearing to not be like their parents though they were not seeking help. I later heard, through my sister, that my parents had indeed attended a couple of ACA meetings but did not agree with the concept of looking towards their childhood for answers.

There are many stages to recovery. It was not healthy for me to stay in the "blame" stage. Blaming is just one step of many. To re-live the past is to acknowledge to myself and others what I had experienced. This caused me great shame, humiliation and embarrassment. It was ugly, sometimes unbelievably scary. But I was not alone.

Having a healthy support system was crucial to my healing. Friends I made in my first survivors of childhood sexual abuse therapy group became dear to me. As we continued socializing together, attending weekend workshops, going to talks, and spending time in nature, we all experienced the joys of recovery. I was so fortunate to live in a time and place that had lots to offer me on my path to recovery. I participated in re-birthing workshops, therapeutic dance workshops, ritual bonfires, primal scream therapy, art therapy, music therapy, singing crystal bowl meditation therapy. Some events were way over my head, but each activity brought me closer to loving myself along with my inner child.

I remember driving home one Monday after a particularly difficult therapy session. I was shaken by a blood curdling scream vibrating inside my car. It took me several seconds to realize that the scream was coming from deep down within me. Childhood scenes were being replayed in my head like flashbacks and they were terrifying. I was feeling and seeing again what had been done to me as a child as I drove seventy miles an hour down the Ventura Freeway. The thought that saved me was the knowing that I had already experienced this traumatic abuse; it was not happening in the car. I was slowly learning to come down from the ceiling to look at what I had experienced before and I no longer needed to protect myself. What I needed was to witness the event and acknowledge that this was what happened to me as a four-year-old little girl. Opening up these deep wounds would never be as awful as that initial experience.

It became my mission to see and feel what my inner child had seen and felt. I needed to rescue her, let her know that the abuse was wrong, awful, illegal and most important, not her fault. During inner child therapy work the focus is on reaching back through time to be there for her. To not let her be alone, to tell her about the life she will soon have, to show her how I have learned to take care of her by letting her be a little girl. I told her often how she will get to stay home in her safe place with her little girl toys and dolls. No longer will she be subjected to our father. I told her that I am learning how to be a functioning adult. I was learning to come from my adult self. I was learning to take charge of our life so that she no longer would be required to be in charge in order for us to feel safe. The coping skills she developed before were no longer necessary. She no longer needed to confront my boss, supervise staff, pay the bills, drive the car, have sex, or be the mom. I slowly began to learn how to take care of both of us.

Calm and serene moments in our life were the perfect time for our family to create new coping skills. The most powerful tool that the three of us created were simple lists we posted on our refrigerator. Those lists helped us to focus on taking care of ourselves in loving healthy ways. There was a list of menus with our favorite foods, another was list of restaurants for when we wanted to eat out, and another list of ways to calm down, release stress and regain sanity. Our favorite list was titled "Fun things to do." This list contained lots of activities, such as boogie boarding at the beach, riding bikes, going to the movies, playing in the river and our most favorite was "Sunday drives." Nearly every Sunday we jumped into our car and headed for adventure. We loved nature and exploring her beauty. Once a month, we would go camping for three days. We started out by camping in our car. We graduated to tent camping, then camping in our pop-up camper, then a tent trailer, and eventually camping in our motorhome. These special times we shared helped us to rejuvenate and reconnect with one another during these turbulent times. The three of us have built lifelong memories.

One of the first, most profound groups Ralph and I participated in was a Rebirthing Workshop. We were in a group of about ten people, facilitated by a husband/ wife team. We met at their lovely house on a hill with a large sunken living room below tall, wood-beamed ceilings. Three of the walls were glass and the beautiful old oak trees outside created a lovely dappled, sunlight-filled room. Every person, in turn, shared their intention for what they wanted to release through the workshop. As they shared, the rest of the group sent that person loving energy, giving them strength and support. After each person had shared, we sang songs and chanted. The room had a wonderful essence of healing and acceptance. We then lay down on the beautiful carpets with pillows under our heads, covered in soft blankets. Beautiful music played in the background as the facilitators took us through a guided meditation.

I slowly went deeper and deeper into a dream state in which I was in my mother's belly and aware of what was going on. I realized that my existence was a problem for my parents and their families. They were both very young and unprepared for me. There was guilt and shame surrounding my existence. My birth seemed to be having a negative effect on several lives, as I was not wanted. I was not desired. I did not feel secure in my parents' ability to take care of me. I did not want to come out. I was not going into the correct position to be born. I was in the breech position (butt first) refusing to come out. My experience as a human required my birth. After four hours of labor, I was born vaginally.

Somehow I have picked this life experience, as did my mother and her mother, as well as the mothers before us, which included experiencing sexual abuse. The cutting of the umbilical cord was so traumatic that it left unhealed nerves that cause me to be unable to touch my belly button without a stinging sensation radiating outward. I was born into a world with a just barely fifteen-year-old mother wed to my nineteen-year-old father. Their youth and inexperience was problematic. Their world had suddenly changed.

In one of my therapy groups, we were each to buy a doll that represented our inner child. I had yet to embrace my redheadedness so I bought a bald baby doll. We were to spend time every day for thirty days with our baby. We were to provide a safe area in our house for our baby where we nurtured her and allowed her to be a baby, and this is where she stayed when I went about my daily life doing my adult activities. I practiced being a good mom to her and allowed her to always be a baby. I was the adult now and I was in charge of my life and my decisions. This sounds a lot easier than it really is. It brought up a lot of shit that had been buried for a very long time. One woman was vicious to her baby as she carried her around by her foot. She would throw her across the room, refused to hold her, clean or dress her. This eventually allowed her to see how she was currently treating herself, her inner child, and a possible insight as to how she was treated as a baby.

I am so grateful that Sean was not a girl and that Ralph and I chose not to have children, as we may have had a daughter, triggering a nightmare of reactions from me. I hear stories of women who physically or emotionally abandon their newborn daughters. They have breakdowns or are abusive to these small helpless baby girls who, in the mother's eyes, represent the vulnerable innocent needy baby the mother once was. Having intimate knowledge of what can happen to an innocent child can cause an eruption of fears, anxieties, insecurities, abandonments, and helplessness. These mothers are simply projecting their fears onto their precious babies. This happened to me, my mother, and my grandma. It would have been a terrible thing to pass on to

107

another young innocent baby girl. I would never have been able to trust Ralph to even hold her, let alone change her diaper or bathe her. I would have been unable to trust any man with this baby girl. Seeing me in her would not have triggered nurturing, protective and loving actions from me. On some level, the Universe and I knew this. I was lucky to have never been put to the test. I did try as best I could to protect my sisters from our father and mother, though I don't know if I will ever know their truths. I still don't know what my father may have done to them, once I left the house at seventeen. In turn, each one of us left our parents' house before finishing high school.

Doing inner child work was difficult for me at first. I was in a group setting and the therapist asked us to visualize our inner child. In my mind's eye, I saw my little sister Ruth as a baby. I could not connect with my inner child. I didn't understand why my inner child was Ruth and not me; this frightened me. Why was I bringing up images of her instead of me? I knew that I had tremendous guilt about the way I treated Ruth as a child and how I had been cruel and jealous of her. I became so fearful and filled with shame that I left that group.

The following therapy group was where we used the baby dolls to connect with our inner child. This helped me to focus on myself first. The guilt with Ruth was very overwhelming. I could have easily focused on that behavior, giving me yet another reason to hate myself or shut down. I realized that I needed to be as healthy as possible before I took on the task of healing my relationship with Ruth. It was challenging to maintain my focus on my healing. There were a million distractions, causes that I could get lost in, available to take my focus away from my own healing.

Taking up a cause outside of me was very admirable and socially acceptable. Instead of focusing on contributing to the world's healing process, I needed to heal myself first. I needed tools to help me deal with everyday life. I needed and desired to stay alive. I had quit the cigarettes, drugs and alcohol, yet I was still filling up my time with being busy. I harnessed this energy to help me deal with my daily chores, work, maintaining a household, gardening, being a wife and mother and most importantly, on my recovery.

I was introduced to the concept that time may not be linear, which allowed me to be in the present, while reaching back to the past. One technique that I assimilated into my toolbox was the practice of reaching back, as an adult, to my inner child and comforting her, holding her and loving her. I would tell her how much she was loved and was not to blame for what was happening to her. I told her that one day it would all stop, and that we would seek help and learn to recover from the abuse. I let her know that she would grow up to be a loving, responsible and healthy woman.

I expanded on this theory and found myself being able, in the present, to be comforted by my future self as I went through this devastating healing process. I could feel my wise crone self; white haired and wrinkled, embracing me, telling me that everything was going to be okay, that I would be okay and slowly I would become a better person, creating a better life. This gave me security in the knowledge that I was doing the right thing for myself and helped to keep me alive. This practice was particularly helpful during the initial period of my choice to divorce my parents.

I learned in one of my self-help books about toxic parents. My parents were toxic to my very being. Another favorite self-help book asked me to examine how I felt after visiting with my family. I always felt terrible after a visit with them. I would feel sickened and shamed and I searched for a way to numb those feelings. Whenever all of us girls gathered, with our men, at our parents' house, the men would drink too much. They too did not feel comfortable. My sisters and I did not drink nor smoke in front of our parents and we couldn't wait to leave so we could light up and have a beer. I have great difficulty with people who tell me that all I need to do to heal is to forgive my parents. Frequently I ask them, "What if Hitler had had children, would you also ask them to forgive their father?" Most people shake their heads and say "Oh, of course not" and I tell them "Well, it is the same for me!"

As young adults, my sisters and I were best friends. We spent our weekends together along with our loved ones. Our get-togethers were usually parties of drinking, drugging, and letting loose. We had grown up in such a restricted, controlled and somber environment and, once we left home, we were nearly out of control. We wanted to try everything and most things we tried numbed us from our truth. When we were together, our synergy somehow recreated the dynamics of our childhood. Our gatherings brought fear, loss of control, and the feeling of impending violence. In our altered states, we manifested scenarios affirming what our parents told us, that we were no good, unreliable, incompetent, less than, and worthless.

After I divorced my parents, their family gatherings took place at our parents' house. Lynn had moved out of the state and our parents paid for her and her two boys to spend time with them every summer. In the following ten years, I saw Lynn and her boys only a couple of times. I would sometimes get word of her visits, but most of the time I did not hear from her at all. The four of us girls were not together again for nearly twenty-five years.

Jean and I had married best friends. I thought of myself as my sister's "good" mother, filling in for my mother by essentially spying for my parents. I was also controlling, demanding, prying and interfering in Jean's life. I worked nearby and would spend my lunch hour with her baby boy until Jean returned home from work. I loved spending this time with my nephew but, as soon as my sister got home, I became the inquisitor. I was constantly checking to see if she had taken my sage advice from the previous day. I was pumped up with ego and pride and was relentless in my quest to tell her how to live her life. I had her under a microscope. It must have been hell for her.

After one of my lunchtime lectures with her, I returned to work, so proud of myself that I told my co-worker of my wonderful words of wisdom which I had spewed out once again to my little sister. My co-worker shook her head, looked at me and, with kindness in her heart, said "Would any of your sisters talk to you like that?" The words hit me hard; she was right. I was abusing my authority as the big sister. I was being cruel and this made me feel awful. My sisters would never talk to me like this. I should never have treated them in such a manner. I was using them, along with their lives, to escape the truth about mine. I was to the point of obsession. I enjoyed spending my lunches with my nephew and sisters so I tried to use some restraint. This proved to be more difficult than I had imagined.

Sometimes our sister Ruth would join us for lunch. One lunch get together, Ruth arrived at Jean's house before the rest of us, only to find the teenage babysitter naked in the crib with our eighteen-month-old nephew, who was also naked,. Ruth made her leave. We were beside ourselves, not knowing what to do. We hurriedly went to the park to get away from the "scene of the crime." We stayed at the park for a short while and then we walked back to Jean's house. When Jean's husband arrived home we told him what had happened. He went to the babysitter's house to talk to the family. The parents of the sitter told Jean's husband that the girl had been sexually molested by her uncle and would not be returning.

As I watched Jean, along with her husband, pull together as a family to try to deal with this, I realized I needed to stop interfering with their lives. They showed me how adult they were, that they did not need me to tell them what to do. I needed to focus on myself, which proved to be harder than I thought it would. I was not able to vocalize to them what was going on with me so I slowly withdrew. I didn't know how to act properly, so I began to monitor myself. I started to put into play the phrase my mother used to love to frequently repeat to us which was "If you don't have anything nice to say then don't say anything at all." Since I was not used to saying or hearing "nice things," I shut down. Shortly afterward, Ruth left California. We spoke only three times during the following twenty years.

Jean's family had now grown with the birth of their beautiful daughter. I loved spending time with my nephew and niece. I was my best self with them. I was someone who I could love and be proud of. I didn't know where I kept this other me but it truly gave me hope that I was not all bad. Often Ralph and I would take them to the park, the movies, or to the beach. Every week I looked in the newspaper for a children's activity in town for us to do. We had a lot of fun with them. Ralph and I no longer partied on the weekends with Jean and her husband. They were having marriage difficulties, leading us to distancing ourselves from them. This left Jean feeling abandoned by me. After several months, Jean wrote me a letter saying that it was too hard for her to feel rejected by me, that she would no longer allow me to spend time with her children. I was devastated and hurt, yet I knew it took a lot of courage for her to write that letter. I did not have the courage to challenge the letter. I could not even bring myself to talk to her about it. I froze every time I thought about discussing this with her. I had recently divorced my parents and felt all alone in dealing with this.

Jean did not explain any of this to her children. On the weekends, her kids would call me to ask if they could spend time with me. I was at a loss for words. I told them that they would have to ask their mother if it was okay, but it was never okay. The whole thing was a huge fucking mess and for the next ten years, I saw them maybe half a dozen times. Sadly, I was no longer a part of their youth or teenage years.

Eventually Jean and her husband divorced; Jean's daughter lived with her and their son lived with his dad. I understand that it was very difficult on the kids and I wish I could have been there for them, as well as for Jean. Several years later, Jean took up playing the violin again joining a popular all-female band in town. Ralph and I decided that we wanted to see her play, so we went to one of their fund-raising performances. She played well and seemed happy to see us. We went to a couple of their performances and we tried to get caught up on each other's lives but it was strained.

A year later, I saw her in the grocery store and it was good to see that we both had improved our ability to purchase groceries in a normal fashion. She was unhappy that her daughter had moved to Vermont to be near her boyfriend's parents, but she was also hopeful that they would return. Jean had a good job, played her violin and had a new boyfriend. I later learned that she and her boyfriend lived just down the street from us. For six months I had unknowingly walked past her house every morning on my daily walks. Knowing that she was just on the other side of the front door of their house as I passed broke my heart.

Ruth was now back and living with our parents. Jean's daughter had returned from Vermont and had just given birth to a baby boy. As I drove past Jean's house, I could see them all visiting in her front yard. Seeing my sisters, their families and my parents gathered at her house for BBQ's was tearing me apart. I so missed being with my sisters. They were the best friends I ever had.

That summer, I received a call from Ruth saying that Lynn was coming to visit and would I like to join them for dinner at a local Mexican restaurant, the same one where I had worked when I was sixteen. I was overjoyed. The four of us had not been together in twenty-five years and I had not seen Lynn for almost ten years. I was so excited that I left work early and was waiting for them at the restaurant. I held my breath as they walked through the front door. I began to shake and cry; I was so happy to see us all together once again. We were all in our fifties and, just like old times, we all talked at once, even finishing each other's thoughts.

I was hurt to find out that Ruth, along with Jean, had driven to the airport to pick up Lynn. I had not been invited to join them.

It was becoming evident that I was the outsider, but I was so happy to be there that I pushed the hurt aside. It was awkward, yet exhilarating, to be together once again.

A couple of days later, I invited them all to come to my house for dinner. We had moved to a cabin in the woods along a creek with a common area containing a BBQ area, volley ball area and clubhouse. The clubhouse was built in the twenties. It was a large wooden structure with windows, creaky wooden floors, and a rock fireplace. The furniture was leftovers from those who had updated their cabins. Most of the chairs and couches were overstuffed upholstered dinosaurs from the past, which the rats and mice loved, having made comfy condos of them all. There were ping-pong tables and shuffleboard diagrams painted on the floor. The four of us had a great time.

As children, we had a ping-pong table and a pool table. Grandma Jane loved to haunt the pool bars in the beach community she lived in. One Christmas, she bought us all a pool table. We kept it in the garage and we became instantly popular.

The wine was flowing and our mouths were running. We replayed old stories, asking each other questions that had plagued us for some time "Did you sleep with my husband while we were dating?" "Did you really go out with so and so?" "Where did you go that night?" We laughed and cried into the wee hours of the morning. I loved spending time with my three sisters as old wounds were mending and new ones were addressed. Lynn was in town for another week and I was looking forward to us spending more time together.

Ruth called me three days later to say they all were going thrift store shopping the next day and would I like to join them. I was thrilled. I made arrangements with work to take the day off. We had shopped at thrift stores since we were young and loved the adventure. The selections of clothing were beyond anything a mall could provide and the prices were unreal. It was exciting finding new treasures, often purchasing some divine new item that could transform a room. I normally shopped by myself, and I was so looking forward to shopping with my sisters. Ruth said they would pick me up at 11 am. At 11:15 am she called to say that they had gotten an early start, had already finished all their shopping, were eating lunch, and were then heading home. I was crushed, but I said nothing. They had made their choices and I felt that whatever I had to say wouldn't change the fact that they chose to eliminate me from their plans.

On the last day of Lynn's visit, Ruth called to invite us to a BBQ at Jean's house. I swallowed my hurt pride and went. I learned that, the day before, Sean had taken them all to the beach to ride on his jet ski. They had been spending every free day at the beach; again, I was not invited. At the BBQ they told me that Sean was riding two of them on the jet ski when he lost control and ran into a woman who was lying on the beach. She was hurt, though not badly. I went into a rage, saying how stupid that was of them and what were they thinking - on and on I ranted. I sounded like our parents all wrapped into one person. As I heard my castigations vibrating throughout the room and saw the look on everyone's face, I soon realized one reason why they avoided me; it was because of me.

I was back living in our childhood environment, terrified of the consequences of us "being bad". I was angry thinking they had put us all back into that situation and now they had dragged Sean

116

into this pit with us. I was again a little girl terrified of our parents' anger. A part of me thought that, if I yelled loud enough, this would all go away. I finally calmed down and apologized, explaining to them that I was being triggered when the four of us were together. It felt like our childhood all over again, as if a dark cloud consumed us like an evil entity. It felt like we were evil bad girls, so evil that bad things were bound to happen to us. It was an awful feeling and explained why we had been apart for all those years.

When we were attending ACA (Adult Children of Alcoholics) meetings, a few people began to share about sexual abuse that they had suffered as children. A group of us with these issues formed a "family of choice" and we became a loving and supportive family unit. We spent holidays together, creating the environment that felt right to us. We used each other for support and became fast friends. We had heard about a new 12-step meeting group called SIA, Survivors of Incest Anonymous. The meetings were for survivors of sexual abuse who were seeking recovery. We found a small group being held in a New Age bookstore. Our little group grew and grew until we outgrew our little storefront meeting space. Eventually we found a large meeting area inside a local church that was willing to allow us to meet for free. The group swelled to forty members. It became so large that we had to split the meeting in half so all would have a chance to share.

We met once a week and afterwards a group of us would gather at the local coffee house and talk about how our lives were changing since joining SIA. We supported each other in many ways. For many, these group members were the only people who knew their shameful secrets. Most of us had therapists, as the meeting literature suggested, but we found it very important and helpful to have a life outside of the therapist's walls.

A group of twenty of us decided that we would like to start a writing workshop using the "Courage to Heal" book and workbook. We split into two families, meeting every Monday evening. Every week we worked on a chapter and shared what we had written. It was healing to have a group that listened to my answers and for me to listen to others as they shared theirs. It was not easy doing this "work" but it was very therapeutic and magic did happen.

There were suggested activities in the workbook that we all enjoyed doing. We made several collages. Some represented how we felt on the inside, others represented what had happened to us, and others represented what we wanted in our future. We made plaster masks of our faces. We made fabric art pieces of our handprints that were sent to the National Sexual Abuse Quilt project to be incorporated into the national quilt. We made "God boxes" using shoe boxes that we decoupaged inside and out keeping favorite items safely inside. Later we began going to the movies together, having bonfires on the beach, roller skating, Valentine's Day parties, and even spending the holidays together. As we did the arduous painful inner child work in the writing workshop, we rewarded ourselves with fun youthful activities as a way to balance the energy and experience joy as we crept forward on our path to recovery. Through these group experiences, I learned what trust felt like, how to be present during conflicts and to accept other's judgment.

The mask-making project was about trust. In the beginning, trusting my writing workshop family was very scary. The mask making consisted of covering my face in Vaseline, lying down on the floor while my friends placed layers of warm goopy gauze across my face with openings left for my nostrils so I could breathe. They placed layer upon layer until finished. I laid there for an hour as the plaster dried. They then removed the plaster mask. Once it was off, I had to gain the courage to actually look at the likeness of myself. We then placed clay inside the mask to make a realistic impression of ourselves. This process yielded a mask very similar to a death mask as there is no expression captured.

I looked at my solemn face, unadorned, without color and I found that I soon began to feel kindness towards this face, eventually cherishing this physical reproduction of myself. On Valentine's Day, we all gathered at our house with our plaster casts. We decided to make art with our likenesses. I took a blank cloth canvas, covered it in gesso, then while it was still wet, I placed my mask on the canvas, securing the edges with gesso. When the gesso was dry, I painted the whole canvas and mask creating a cloud effect. I secured a few feathers to the top of the mask. Years earlier, I had purchased a pair of earrings at an art faire in town. They had been made by a lovely woman and her young daughter. One of the earrings eventually broke but I had saved the unbroken one in my jewelry box. I placed the earring on the art piece where my ear would have been. A couple of years later at my women's group meeting, I brought this art piece to share. It was then that I discovered that one of my dearest friends in the group was the same lady that had made the earrings. When she saw the earring she assumed that I had bought it at a thrift store and, when I told her that I had bought them from her, I could see her body shift ever so slightly as she stood a little taller and smiled with her eyes as she took pride in her creation, which was now part of my creation.

In the 1980's, my work environment was training us how to make quick judgments and how to effectively utilize every minute of the day. We were being taught a 2-minute judging rule where we quickly sized up people and situations so as not to waste valuable time. I was very good at this, as I could spot peoples' faults immediately, always finding a reason to keep them at a distance. I believed that, if I didn't let you in, I didn't need to trust you and you couldn't hurt me. This gave me permission to not like you and this was a way to protect myself. In my mind, the act of protecting me was the only way to keep alive. If I didn't let you, in you could neither hurt me nor see just how damaged I was. I desperately needed to keep people away. I felt so shameful, dirty, disgusting, worthless, evil, dirty, dirty...dirty. So dirty that I did not wear white as I felt my very essence would stain the fabric. I believed that the abuse had tainted my skin. This feeling was multi-level. I wouldn't let you near enough to see how bad I was. I believed there were people who could sense that I was damaged and could see through me.

As a child, I discovered that, if I blurred my vision when my parents or other scary adults looked at me, I was less scared or intimidated. When I learned that the eyes are considered the mirrors of the soul, I tried very hard to not have eye contact with people as they would be able to see my dirty broken soul. As an adult, blurring my vision helped me deal with my bosses and also allowed me to slowly, very slowly, learn how to look someone in the eye and let them look into my eyes. This allowed me to relax and focus on the other person. Initially, I hated the one-on-one therapeutic technique where people are paired off and spend time looking straight into each other's eyes. I was the one who always voted against doing this practice, yet I wound up being the person who cried the hardest. I also began to empathize and connect with the other person as they shed tears. It became a very powerful technique in breaking down my barriers that I had built to prevent others seeing me.

I also dreaded the mirror therapy technique where the practice was to look into the mirror at my own eyes, then to tell myself that I love myself. We were to do this each day for 30 days. It was a very painful process. As I slowly began to connect with myself, I started to feel love and empathy for myself. Later I graduated to standing naked in front of the mirror, learning to really see myself and declaring love for every part of my body. This is a really tough one that I am still working on.

I still have feelings of devastation at the loss of my family. I truly desire to be loved and supported by loving parents, but they are not those people. It hasn't been easy when my co-workers asked what I did for my mother on Mother's Day, father on Father's Day. I recoiled with shame punishing myself for being a bad daughter. My sisters began referring to relatives as "My aunt, my cousin, and my grandmother". I didn't want to be the outsider of my family but I was, as relatives became "their" relatives, not mine. I was treated as if I had divorced myself from my entire family.

When my Grandma Jane died, I received a message on my answering machine from my sixteen-year-old niece. The message said "Hi Auntie, I'm calling because your Grandma Joan, Jane, Jean, whatever her name was, died last week and I thought you'd like to know, bye." There was no obituary and no trinkets of hers passed down to me.

While reading my morning paper, I discovered that one of my cousins had died. Her father and my father were brothers and we cousins had grown up together. The only time I had seen her as an adult was six months earlier in a mall parking lot. She was frail, having trouble walking, and my aunt was helping her get out of the car. The Universe had given me a chance to visit with her but I failed to take that opportunity. As they walked to the store, I drove away. I decided that I must attend her funeral. I was working with a young woman whose husband was very close to the family; he had grown up next door to them. I knew she and her husband would be attending the funeral along with others from my childhood. This gave me the courage to attend.

My father and his two brothers had very tenuous relationships, on again, off again. During this time period, their friendship was off, making our attendance even easier. I had had no contact with my parents for over twenty years. As we arrived, my parents literally clung to the walls as Ralph and I circulated around, visiting with family and friends for the first time in decades. My cousin's family was there, but none of our other cousins or my sisters attended. My Grandma Lee was there and we were very happy to see each other.

My cousin had been born with diabetes and fought with her father constantly about her health and how she neglected herself. Apparently she had married someone he did not approve of and they had decided to have a child, even though the doctors said it

122

would kill her. Her son was now ten years old and autistic. Her husband had recently been in a car crash, suffering brain injuries, making this a very sad situation.

My cousin, along with her husband, knew she was dying and they had planned out their future actions. She chose to be cremated and have her ashes spread in her favorite place, the ocean. Her father thought that was a horrible idea, that her mother would not have a place to visit and so demanded to have her buried in the local cemetery. My cousin had had a very strained relationship with her parents. I know where that came from as I grew up with her. I saw my uncle take control, then demand his way just as I had seen my father, his older brother, do. I knew my father would also demand control of us even in death, hence strengthening my decision to divorce them.

I was nearly cut off entirely from my family. I found out on Facebook that my niece had given birth to a baby girl. I miss being with my sisters and being included as one of them. When they visit, it feels as though they are on a fact-finding mission directed by my parents. Ralph had given Sean an Indian arrowhead which he had been given by his grandfather. My parents have been collecting arrowheads for decades and now my sisters showed up at our house wanting to know where the arrowhead came from, did we have more, on and on. I could hear my father's voice coming from their mouths and this sickened me.

Even though I chose to extricate myself from my parents, it still saddens me. It was not an easy choice to make. For years, I would dream that I forgave them, that we were a family once again. In my dreams, my act of forgiveness changed everything; we were all healed and life was wonderful. Those dreams haunted me so much that I started to plan our reunion. Even though I was scared and nervous, I told myself that this was the right thing to do. I was guilty of breaking one of the Ten Commandments, to Honor and Love thy Parents. The so-called experts said that forgiving them was the only way I would find peace and happiness. One doctor I went to in order to get a prescription refilled for anti-anxiety medication asked why I took them, I told him that I suffered from anxiety due to childhood incest. He refused to write the Rx. He told me that I needed to forgive and invite Jesus into my heart. I was made to feel that not only was I blatantly going against the experts, now I was denying Jesus.

Several times I planned and plotted our reunion. Each time that I was ready to contact them; I would receive word of something they had done that was so ridiculous or mean that I dropped my plans for reconciliation. I now feel that the Universe was protecting me from them. I believe that my forgiveness will take place when I am ready and not a minute sooner. Forgiveness is not a goal I strive to achieve. Being alive, healthy and sane is my first priority and my main focus. Forgiveness will be a wonderful by-product reward that I will attain as the result of my hard work. My biggest job is forgiving myself for what happened to me and accepting that I was a helpless, defenseless, innocent tiny girl when my father began sexually molesting me. I grew to be a tender, scared, broken teenager who certainly didn't deserve to be molested, raped, beaten, neglected or tortured at the hands of Jack. I now must learn to forgive myself for being me, by holding this truth in my heart and mind.

Dreams often played an important part of my healing. As a child I had several recurring nightmares. One was of an immense grizzly bear that would pull my hair and chase me. It was terrifying. The second one was of a massive tidal wave that was constantly threatening me and my sisters. Later, when I took a dream therapy class, I realized the meanings of these dreams. The grizzly bear in my dream was my father who was constantly pursuing me. Due to the constant sexual abuse I suffered, my emotions were slowly being released into my dreams, manifesting as huge waves trying to drown me and my sisters.

I also had the strange dream of searching for a toilet only to find toilets that were completely full of shit, so full that I was unable to even hover over them to pee. I think of these dreams as my life being shit that would not disappear down into the sewage drain. I felt that my basic humanness was causing me so much discomfort that I was not finding a way to release it. This was reminiscent of my mother locking me out of the house where the toilet resided, forcing me to use our yard or the gas station next door.

Once I started going to school, I had recurring dreams of being in school naked from the waist up. I would be exposed to all the other students, fearing that they would see what a bad person I thought I was. This is commonly believed to be the result of feeling exposed, vulnerable and powerless. I had this dream hundreds of times and, upon awaking, I always felt depressed. For years, I felt that I had no control over these dreams. The humiliation, combined with the lack of control these dreams represented, caused me great distress. Through recovery I decided that I would be proactive, trying to assist myself as best I could. I wanted to try to change the direction of this dream. Before falling asleep, I would prepare myself by imagining that I could assist myself with a sweater. I imagined that the sweater would be with me in my dream and I could use the sweater to cover myself up. In the dream, the sweater had a mind of its own and always managed to slip away from me and disappear. It looked like I was undressing instead of covering up.

This happened over and over again. I thought that maybe the sweater was too heavy, so the next thing I tried was to add a blouse tucked under my arm. The blouse turned out to be slippery and, when I wasn't paying attention, it also would fall away and disappear and again, I would be topless. When this happened, I would shield my breasts with my arms or my school books but then seconds later I would find my breasts unprotected for everyone to see. I planned to take a scarf with me the next time I had this dream. I had tucked the scarf into my pocket and felt prepared. When I found myself topless, I used the scarf to wrap around my bust but now I looked like I had intentionally dressed this way for school with the scarf so sheer that I looked even worse. This dream recurred until I was close to forty years old, though in the dream I am always a teenager.

The work I was doing started to have a positive effect on my dreams. I was working on incorporating my Anima/Animus personas, my male and female parts of myself. I had done collage work to create my interpretation of what my Animus would look like. I had even led a workshop on creating an Animus soul card. I created a card with wonderful depictions of the male aspect. It contained a picture of Einstein and a photo of a young man that looked like someone I had met as a teenager. The young man was with some friends in a van parked along the beach. They had just finished surfing and invited my girlfriend and me to join them in the van to smoke a joint. We all sat in the van, with the door open, getting high. I talked with this beautiful young man for a short time before they needed to leave. They were very sweet young men who were non-threatening and very kind to us. I also included a picture of a snow-covered volcano that represented the strong male, along with his seed. The card also contained pictures of daredevils doing amazing feats. This card, to me, represented all that was good about the males in the world.

This was the beginning of a huge chunk of healing for me, which helped me in accepting the goodness of the masculine energy within me. I was becoming a Warrioress and desired to be balanced within myself by incorporating all that was available to me if I was ever to be the whole person that I sought to be.

Shortly after making my animus card, the naked dreams returned and I realized that I needed to work with this dream to heal my wounded self. In my next naked dream a beautiful young man entered. In my time of need, he came to my side and placed his jacket around me. He then wrapped his arm around my shoulders and took me away from the school environment. I was being protected from feeling vulnerable, shamed and powerless as I was magically transformed. I was wearing a beautiful blue ball gown from the forties and he was wearing the most elegant black silk suit. We began dancing a beautiful waltz, twirling and spinning with perfection and ease. The air around us began to crystalize with color and light while we began to levitate. We slowly rose higher and higher. As we twirled, colors surrounded us like the most beautiful and gentle vortex reaching to the heavens. Slowly he and I became one. He was my Animus, my male aspect of myself; he was beautiful and good and now I owned that part of me. I felt protected, secure and safe now that I had accepted my male side, allowing him to be present in my life. I have never had the naked dream again. I feel that this is one of the most important healings I have achieved and a large part of why I had chosen to have this human experience on earth.

Another horrible recurring dream that needed to be transformed involved Jack. For nearly ten years after our divorce, on nearly a weekly occurrence, I dreamt that I was still married to him, having never obtained my divorce. In the dream he would once again be beating and raping me. I would wake up in a terrified and depressed state, believing the dream to be true. It would take several minutes for me to realize it was just a dream, but it still would haunt me all day. I feared that somehow the dream was a premonition or that my actual life was the dream and I would wake up back in hell once more.

Once I was married to Ralph, I thought this nightmare would go away but, in the dream, Ralph would turn into Jack. Slowly I began to realize that I could work with this dream, much like I had with the naked dream. I was able to program myself to scream when having this nightmare. My screaming would violently wake me up out of the nightmare. I enjoyed this success but it was very traumatic for Ralph. Luckily Sean is a heavy sleeper and never heard me.

Once I felt out of danger of being sucked back into that old life with Jack, I began to place weapons in my dream to protect myself. On several occasions in these dreams, Jack used the weapons, guns and knives, against Ralph, Sean and I. After years of working on this nightmare, Ralph appeared in my dream with a large pair of scissors where he managed to stab Jack, who then quickly died, never again to haunt my sleep.

Some of my dreams have been very epic in the importance they have had on my life. These dreams were so significant that I have created collages that represent them. Dream collages are a way to deeply connect with soul through the healing that dreams can bring. As I made my dream collages the dream suddenly became alive. I began to remember more and more of the dream as I selected pictures that represented what I saw and felt. In doing so, the multi-layered messages were easier to recognize. On one such occasion the dream represented the genetic history of my ancestors which lives within me. The dream included castles and ships with craggy beach fronts surrounded by gloomy weather. Ralph had quite a collection of art books and in a crazed moment I tore through the books pulling out pages that represented my dream. I sat on the living room floor with desecrated books and torn pages of exactly what I had dreamt. I taped several large pieces of poster boards together and recreated that very important dream. I felt that my ancestors had visited me in my dream. As I was amongst them, I felt, tasted and smelled my former life. I realized just what history flowed in my veins, how strong I was and how supported I felt.

In the dream, I was a part of a clan that lived in castles built on the edge of very steep cliffs overlooking a wild and dangerous sea. In the dream, I had decided to leave my clan. As I was preparing to leave, I was reassured that my clan would slay the demons that had haunted me all my life, and maybe many lives. I was extremely strong and capable and trusted to make the journey. There was a ship full of men to assist me; it was loaded with all the provisions I needed to set out into my new life. My clan had taught me well and provided me with inner and outer tools to continue on with my difficult journey of recovery. They cheered me on and still do. I can feel them when I have a victory. They are with me when I stand tall, when I say my truth and when I am helpful to others who are also struggling with their journey. They are with me as I encourage those who are fighting to be alive. I have since felt a deep connection to that person/me who decided to venture out.

Ten years have passed, and I am experiencing a bit of a crisis dealing with moving away from my home country and being disinherited from my parents. This crisis is affecting me as I write this book and I asked the Universe to bring to me a wise woman for counsel. I search for an old crone and what I find is a woman my age. It is then that I realize that I, too, am of crone age and ready to use my experience and gifts that I have accumulated. This wise woman is deeply connected to the feminine and is exactly what I need. After thirty minutes of background as to what brought me to seek her out and what I needed to heal, she took me through a guided meditation. She had me begin by imagining that I was standing in the front of a line of my maternal ancestors as they lined up behind me. I turned to look at them and found the similarities between us. What I noticed was that they all were very strong, opinionated and capable women, whether they used those traits or not. They were not women you would want to mess with. They were Warrioresses. They were not meek and no one would ever call them door-mats.

I was born into this tribe to learn how to be fearless, not to learn how to comb my hair, put on makeup, or be beguiling. It was never part of my destiny to stay within my birth family. I then saw

130

myself joining the ranks of men and women who were also victims/survivors of sexual abuse. I started to see myself standing amongst them, within the ranks of the wounded, when I realized that is not what my birth-right brought me here to do. I needed their energy, drive, bravery, and determination. I am to LEAD theses armies and WIN battles. I am a thriver. I am an example of what thirty years of healing, reaching out and fighting for my survival can result in. I am that woman who climbed onto that ship to seek out my destiny and I have found it.

The beauty and magic of creating collages is that, as time passes, their meaning becomes deeper and more profound. Dreams come to us over and over again until we can recognize the lesson. They can teach us to be discerning in what we ask for, how to be clear and how to look at all possible situations and outcomes. All of these skills can become very helpful in our everyday life.

One dream that I have yet to reconcile is a dream I have had since I was probably five or six. This dream takes place in the late fifties-early sixties so I don't believe it came from any suggestions in my waking hours. This dream is set in the countryside dotted with white cottages and thatched roofs on low rolling green hills with sheep grazing in the meadows. Soon this scene switches to a metropolitan city with skyscrapers grouped together. As far as the eye can see, there are layers upon layers of every kind of flying machine possible, all moving in slow motion, in all directions. The drone of the engines is almost deafening. The magnitude of the number of flying machines is claustrophobic. Everyone just stands there in awe of what is above them as we are all unaware of whose vehicles these are, why they are in the sky or if we are in any danger.

Not too long ago, I have seen three movies that accurately depict what I saw in my dreams. I am unsure of the significance this dream has in my life or what the message or lesson is. I do know that one of my favorite sounds is the low hum of a single or twin engine small plane.

One job I had was located on a small runway and, for lunch, I loved to take walks along the runway, listening to the planes take off and land. This dream may be just a past memory or it may have come from the future, I still don't know yet.

SOULTHRIVER

CHAPTER SIX

Our town was known around the state for the great thrift stores we had. Shopping at thrift stores soon became my favorite hobby. In a thrift store, I found a wider selection than anywhere else. I found clothes and fabrics that I had never seen before. I would shop most weekends for clothes to wear to work the following week. My wardrobe became a revolving collection of unique clothing. I was constantly cleaning my closets to make room for my newest additions. I brought bags of clothes for donations as I entered the stores. On more than one occasion, I accidentally re-bought what I had previously donated.

I experimented with layering and combining clothing. I had great successes but also huge failures but, being a redheaded blue-eyed lefty, I was used to being stared at, no matter what I was wearing. Shopping at thrift stores requires a close look at what you're buying; you must examine the zippers to see that they are working, check the crotches for rips and give it a good looking over for stains and holes. One blouse I purchased stole my heart as the fit was incredible, the fabric soft as a kitten, the color divine. This one had slipped my careful inspection. Once I was home admiring my new purchases, I noticed a hole and was crushed, I knew that I would never find a blouse like this again. I looked through my sewing notion box where I came across a beautiful tiny lace flower doily. I sewed the doily over the hole with a beautiful result and I began altering my clothes to make them uniquely mine. I had a simple pink vest that had become too small for me and, going back to my bell bottom days, I opened up the side seams and inserted diagonal stripes of various fabrics, and the vest fit perfectly. I loved the look of Levi jackets but they never fit me right. If I could button the jacket, then the arms were too big. I found a beautiful rayon blouse made of a small cabbage rose print. I cut the arms off of both the jacket and the blouse and then sewed the blouse sleeves onto the jacket. I exchanged collars and appliqued small pieces of the blouse fabric into the rectangular areas of the front of the jacket. I had a collection of beautiful labels the fashion houses were attaching to their clothing and I sewed some onto the front and back of the jacket. What I now had was a work of art.

I had a great job supervising an office with accounting staff where I felt free to experiment with what I wore. I can't say that I had a certain style; I liked to try almost anything. I was the only female on the second floor, where sometimes I think I stupefied management, as most of them wore uniforms. I truly stuck out amongst the crowd.

I loved my job. I had a male boss and my job required that I spend a lot of time with him. During our time alone, my mind would create all sorts of uncomfortable scenarios, always sexual in nature, causing me enough distress that sometimes I couldn't concentrate on what we were discussing. I had convinced myself that he could sense what I was thinking. I was afraid that he would think that I was hoping these fantasies would come true.

Being one-on-one with a male had always been difficult for me and I also had great difficulty dealing with those in authority. Being intimate with a male on a purely platonic level was something that my therapist was helping me with and I was now ready to practice what I had learned with my boss. My boss liked my work and my input and gave me great reviews. Still I had those invasive thoughts crowding my brain, but I was slowly able to push them aside while lowering the volume of my crazy thoughts. I was learning how to function in the workplace whilst I was in therapy. I had the job of my dreams.

When I was interviewed for this particular position they asked if I knew how to work a computer. I had had years of experience with data entry, so I told them I had computer experience but, being able to enter data and being able to operate a computer, were two very different skills. On the first day of my job, I was sitting at my desk unable to figure out how to even turn the computer on. I started to panic, fearful that I would be discovered, so I called Ralph. I was in tears, begging him to please help me. He told me how to turn on the computer and how to access my work programs. I spent all my free time at work learning how to use my computer. I took classes at night so I could become proficient. I even learned how to write computer programs for timekeeping and billing.

I was able to create a new claim form for the employees to use with the public that was exceptionally better than the previous one they had been using. I was implementing a new payroll system. I had taken training courses so I could do my job in all emergency situations anywhere in the world. I had a great support system outside of work. Sean was a junior in High School. I was in great health, jogging every morning, and I started a lunchtime walking group at work. I was taking night courses to become a Fire Inspector and I was just finishing up my last class.

At work, I had discovered that the Insurance Department owed our department over three million dollars in unpaid salaries to our employees who had work-related injuries. I was collecting data, rifling through old time card boxes. I thought ahead by taking my chair with me to collect boxes from the storage closet. The storage area was packed full; the two boxes I needed were just one row back, when I did the ultimate stupid thing that I, as the Safety Officer, had trained my staff not to do. I reached over the first row, grabbing the first box with both hands and placing it onto the chair. As I reached to collect the second box, which had been stacked below the first box, I reached over, leaning down as I lifted it, and turned my body, placing the box onto the chair. I twisted my body to place the box onto the chair and my arms and legs went numb. Then I began having shooting pains down my arms and legs. I started to pass out when a friend walked by and I asked her to call Ralph to come get me. This was not office protocol, my first mistake. I was supposed to contact Personnel and alert them to my injury and allow them to handle it. I was not thinking correctly, having no notion as to what was causing me such pain. I just wanted Ralph.

Ralph arrived in his boss's station wagon and took me to a medical clinic, where the doctor did an anal digit exam and decided that my pain was due to my new vegetarian diet. Ralph and I knew this couldn't be what was causing the problem, so he took me to our chiropractor who gave me an adjustment, then sent me home to rest. I slept on the couch next to the bathroom as I had lost control of my bowels. Most of what happened after that was a blur, as I was in so much pain that it greatly affected my short term memory. I had no recollection of moving boxes before the pain started. In order to deal with the pain, I had chiropractor appointments three times a week followed by MRI's, X-rays, doctors' appointments, forms to fill out, followed by interviews, all a living nightmare.

I suffered three herniated discs and was unable to return to work. I was very concerned about my future. Instantaneously, I was thrown into the hell of Workman's Comp where I had to deal with dishonest doctors and lawyers on both sides. I had an appointment with one doctor, who was supposed to be on my side, in a very exclusive part of the neighboring town. He met with me in his office copy room for ten minutes during his lunch break then wrote his report from that meeting. One Workman's Comp doctor dragged a tool across the bottom of my foot, scraping my skin, to try to disprove my claim of having numb feet. My feet were so numb and cold that I started to wear Ugg boots even during the hot summer, but still my calves and feet were ice cold. My left calf began to shrink. I was in constant pain, day and night.

The Insurance Department that I had discovered owed our department millions of dollars, was now handling my Workman's Comp case. My name was well known in that department. The contracted Workman's Comp specialist they had hired to evaluate me asked me what I had done to that department to be treated so poorly. He even went so far as to tell me that I was underpaid for my position and skills and that, when I recovered, he would like to hire me to run his office.

My second mistake was trying to go back to work part-time. I truly wanted to be well again and to continue working at the best job I ever had. I drove forty minutes to work and back in my stick shift car. By the time I reached the office parking lot, I was in terrible pain. Sometimes I couldn't make it to the building without collapsing in the parking lot. Ralph and I then purchased a car with an automatic transmission that would be easier for me to drive. I hid the pain, as I wanted to keep my job, but my performance was suffering, along with my staff that needed me to be there full time.

After a few months of trying to make things work, I requested psychological help to deal with my situation. During that therapy, the disclosure of my history of being sexually abused was documented. This information was used against me by the lawyers. They stated that, because of the abuse, I was unstable and therefore not a good employee. This made no sense to me as my personnel file was filled with gleaming reports from two different department heads. This was a terrible blow to my self-esteem, as I had been working so hard on recovering from the abuse. I had been doing a fantastic job at work and they labeled me as an undesirable employee, due to the incest.

My doctor told me that working part-time was having an adverse effect on my health and even slowing down my physical recovery. She wrote to my work, telling them that I was no longer able to work even part-time. After six months, my work gave me an ultimatum. I was to return to work full time, now ten hours a day, or be fired. Since I was not able to return, I was fired. I had called my boss several weeks before I received the letter stating I was fired and told him that my doctor said I was unable to return to full time work. He was happy to tell me his good news that he was able to eliminate my position, thereby saving the department enough money to allow him to retire early under the Golden Handshake Program. He was thrilled and wished me luck.

I was devastated to be treated as the bad guy, being told that I was lying about my injury as well as my pain. Even my own lawyer stated that we all succumb to back injuries, so I should just accept that. I was told that my injury was due to my weight, which was not true. I was below the average weight for my height and age. I was also told that my injuries were consistent with someone who was thirty seven years old, which was total bullshit.

Unbeknownst to me, I was followed by a Private Investigator for thirteen months, who filmed me during my arrivals and departures from my house and work. One year after my injury, I requested a disability retirement. The Private Investigator showed the Retirement Board the videos he had taken of me. He stated that, at one point, he was unable to follow me in his car to my doctor's appointment, insinuating that I was trying to avoid him. The judge presiding over my case was hired by the County, the very County I had been working for, for ten years. They had gone over my personnel file with a fine toothed comb. My file contained only favorable reports for the ten years I worked for the County. However, they claimed to have discovered something they said proved that I was a liar, as well as untrustworthy.

On my original application ten years earlier, I had failed to include, amongst the requested list of previous surgeries, that I had had Rhinoplasty (a nose job). Since it was an elected cosmetic surgery, I did not think that it fell into the category of surgeries. I was wrong. This omission resulted in marking me as a liar, a bad employee and unworthy of a medical retirement. I was currently collecting disability, was awarded medical coverage for life but, because I failed to include the nose job, I was no longer a good person or worthy of a disability award. The pain from the injury, the brutal depositions, and the medical exams along with my lack of sleep was making me crazy. I was thrown into a world that was confusing, where I was not prepared to take care of myself. It was if I had awakened one morning into a world that was so foreign to me. I had grown up with a work ethic shoved down my throat. I was expected to rise at 6 am every day and my worth was tied to my chores. Taking care of me, being kind to myself and being nurturing to myself were all thought of as being selfish. As kids, we were punished when caught being selfish or self-centered. Fortunately, I had somewhat of a support system, mostly from my chiropractor. Sadly she passed away in the middle of all this. I also had a wonderful massage therapist from whom I received massages twice a week. Amazingly, the county reimbursed for her services!

Spiritually, I was a mess. My back no longer protected me from my nightmares. As a child, I curled up in my bed trying to protect my vagina from my father and, like a shell; my back was what protected me. It was my back that made me feel tall, strong, competent, and able to function in the outside world. My back gave me the courage to seek therapy. My back held me strong when my heart, legs and gut would give out in grief, fear and flashbacks. My back was there for me when I told my truths. Now it was injured and became my enemy, causing me great pain, lack of sleep, fear of the future, and feeling unprotected. My injury was not visually apparent and many thought I lied about it. How could I protect myself with a damaged support system called my spine? In my mind, I believed that I was being bad, that I was not worthy of any special attention, care or concern. My old programming was rearing its ugly head. How dare I think that I was deserving of any special treatment? I heard the voices in my head yelling at me to pull myself together, stop "faking" an injury and quit drawing attention to myself.

I was being broken down. I could no longer keep busy. I could no longer run from my problems, from people, or away from my story. I had gotten to the point of what in AA is called "White Knuckling" it. Though I knew the lingo, and had done the recommended therapies, I was still alone with myself, hanging on by a thread. I needed to not be isolated with my pain. I needed to not be inside my head all the time. I started relying on others, especially Ralph. This was such a new concept for both of us.

I was stressed out having to deal with court hearings, house visits, a dismissal letter from my job, lack of sleep, isolation, constant pain, weight gain, all bearing down on my mind. Not to mention the constant chatter in my head continually reminding me of what a bad person I was and how I had totally fucked up my life. I wasn't even forty yet and I felt crippled. My mind was relentless. I couldn't remember what the calendar said five minutes after I read it. I had all my appointments listed on the calendar and I had to look at it every hour to make sure that I wasn't forgetting something. This is what chronic stress can do to a person.

I decided that I needed to be proactive with my health and with my injury. I visited the local library and researched everything I could find about my type of injury. I had suffered three herniated discs and the information I found about a herniation of T12 showed that there was a strong chance that, if there were complications during surgery, I could become paralyzed. I decided against surgery, which was my third strike.

I was considered uncooperative as I wouldn't do what the Workman's Comp doctors recommended, which was surgery. My job was at the Headquarters of the local Fire Department and many of the men I worked with had been injured on the job. They had chosen to have the surgeries, and years later, they were getting physically worse, regretting their decision to have had surgery.

Everything was pointing me towards alternative therapies. I regularly visited a chiropractor, massage therapist, and an acupuncturist. I exercised on a cross country skiing machine, walked daily, and took antidepressants. I also took lots of ibuprofen, much more than I should have.

A positive, exciting thing that happened to me during this life-changing event was a book I read. It was recommended to me by a psychic I met at a health faire. The book is called "The Nature of Personal Reality" by Jane Roberts, commonly called the "Seth Book." The book is about an entity called Seth that the author channels. In that book there is a simple suggestion that changed how I dealt with my life-stealing injury. In the book, Seth said to spend just five minutes each day living and acting as if the trauma or drama in my life, i.e. my injury, did not exist. I spent five minutes a day dancing as if my body was without injury and pain free. Those five minutes slowly changed my perception of my own reality. I began to no longer identify as an injured person. I began to distance myself from the insult to my being, pain, disability, shame, and the self-loathing at what I had "done" to myself.

Within those five minutes, I was whole again, competent, worthy of self-love. I felt alive, joyful and hopeful. I was slowly learning how to remove the label that I and others had placed on me. I knew that I was not here on this earth to succumb to my physical limitations. I told myself that losing the best job I ever had must mean that there were greater things in store for me and what they were, I had no clue but I knew that I needed to trust in the Universe.

I thought that I needed to discover my next path, once again thinking, as always, that I was in charge. I went back to the local library and I thumbed through a very large book that contained every job title known at that time. I thought that I needed to choose a career to put all my energy into. Luckily, nothing resonated with me, although I was very disappointed at that time as I was ready to move my new life forward.

After nearly two years of dealing with the changes in my life that had been brought on by my injury, I was slowly recuperating. I no longer had my job and my disability payments had stopped. We were now living on Ralph's income. I often spent my days bouncing between depression and acceptance. I had always been a "take charge kind of gal" and now I was shackled with trying to function in a life that was foreign to me. I was going to the Easter Seal pool for water therapy twice a week, where I was surrounded by senior citizens recovering from surgeries and strokes. We were all there for recuperation but I found no peers in the group. I was lonely and needed to find companions.

My incest issues were being brought forward once again due to my lack of distractions. I attended a talk being given by a therapist about childhood trauma. The therapist talked about people being able to divorce their parents and I knew I found a mentor. His office also provided space for local people to conduct 12-step sexual abuse survivors group. I began attending these meetings and was really getting a lot out of them. It was in this group that I learned that the therapist had a childhood sexual abuse survivors' therapy group. I was interviewed, and when there was an opening I was invited to join. I became a dedicated member for five years. The co-therapist was a wise woman who I quickly admired. Years earlier, a dear friend had recommended his spiritual teacher and he had given me her business card. That card was on my nightstand for years; this was the same woman.

The therapy group was a powerful healing experience and I loved all of the members. Because of the natural intensity of the work being done in these meetings, we all learned to trust each other. We all felt mutual love, yet we found it difficult to be friends outside of the group. As I grew healthier in my recovery, my need for friendships became very important. The co-therapist led a women's group that met twice a month and that is where I found my friends. This was a very powerful spiritual group that relied on Native American and Goddess teachings and beliefs.

I learned how to be outside my thinking mind and how to listen to the spiritual world. I learned how to see the world in a different light. I saw meaning in the messages of everyday life. I began developing my spiritual self and my creative self. I began slowly realizing that everything that happened around me was my own personal experience. I recognized that these experiences can guide, teach, and lead me.

The magic began with rock collecting. My son had brought home my first heart rock, a very large heart shaped rock he had found on the beach that he said made him think of me. Shortly afterwards, I began finding heart rocks everywhere. I found rocks with holes the shape of hearts and rocks with heart shapes on them. On one particularly wondrous day, I was on my morning walk and found several heart shapes. One was an oil drip on black top; another was a spot on the lawn. That day I found hearts everywhere speaking directly to my heart, sending me love and hope as I trudged my painful, righteous, heart-filled path of recovery.

Magic was happening everywhere. As a teenager, I raised an orphaned baby crow that learned to talk by mimicking me, though he talked with an amusing oriental accent. Crow became my totem animal. Crow represented the community that I needed in my life, and I seemed to always be in the company of crows. One summer, we were in the mountains camping with friends. As we sat in our chairs drinking in the beautiful surroundings, I mentioned that I hadn't seen any crows since we arrived that morning. Within five minutes, a solitary crow began to circle the sky above us. I gratefully thanked him for being with me.

When Ralph and I were house shopping, I was standing on the third floor deck of a prospective home, when two crows flew within a foot of my head. They dove down, ascended back up, and then dove over my head again. We did wind up buying that house.

The most magical crow experience I had was one morning on my walk. I came across a large group of crows at the park that were gathered on the ground. There was a sprinkler near them that had been watering the park lawn and, as the water ran off the lawn, it puddled up onto the parking lot area, creating a very large silhouette of a crow in profile. The crows gathering around this image appeared to be absorbed in some kind of other world message.

SOULTHRIVER

CHAPTER SEVEN

One morning, after Ralph left for work, I was lying in bed, once again going through my morning mental ritual as to why I "fucked" up my life and what was in my future. I looked over at my clothes closet, gazing at all the clothes I would never wear to the job I no longer had. Having gained weight, I could no longer wear them. They haunted me, mocking my incompetence, lack of potential and unworthiness. In deep frustration, I slowly climbed out of bed, grabbed a pair of scissors and began, one by one, pulling the clothes off their hangers and cutting them up into pieces, throwing all the pieces into a pile on the floor. I was in an altered state, cutting away. When I was done destroying my wardrobe, I slunk back into bed, covered my head with my pillow and bawled my eyes out. I hadn't paid a lot of money for these clothes, my exclusive thrift store wardrobe but it was what they represented and how they had made me feel. I was no longer living that life, no longer needed a work wardrobe, and I felt lost. I was emotionally, as well as physically, exhausted and fell back to sleep.

When I awoke, I was amazed at what I saw. There on the floor of my closet was a beautiful pile of fabrics, a collage of interesting fabrics of varying colors and textures that, when combined, were stunning, beautiful and exciting. I remembered that I had an old dress pattern, probably fifteen years old, in my sewing machine drawer. I dusted off my sewing machine and began to create. I was familiar with piecing fabric together as, in the past, I had made an entire quilt by hand, but this was different. I laid pieces of fabrics on top of each other, folding the raw edges under then top stitching pieces together in pleasing, flattering geometric angles. I added hints of old lace collars here and there. I then created each pattern piece separately, making four long pieced-together triangles for the skirt part of my new dress that created a beautiful handkerchief hem. I designed a flowing dress with a slimming silhouette. The results were beautiful and magical, like nothing I had ever seen before. When I put this creation on, I felt transformed.

My girlfriends from my women's circle were meeting downtown for lunch and I wore my new creation. My dress was the talk of the town. I overheard women talking about "that" dress they had seen that was so beautiful and they wanted to own one. One of my girlfriends was selling her jewelry at the local artisans' faire in two months and she invited me to join her. She was a very well-known artist in the community and she got me approved, sight unseen, as a vendor.

First thing I needed to do was to dive into the local thrift stores to buy clothes made with interesting fabrics. This was so much fun because, even if the clothes didn't fit me or weren't in perfect condition, they could still be used. I happily purchased cart loads of clothes-women's, men's and children's-it didn't matter. My mood brightened greatly. I now had a way to make art and money, helping me to focus on something other than my pain and unhappiness. I started the process of deconstructing the clothes, as I cut the clothes apart creating large pieces of fabric, saving all the buttons and trims. I began to place the fabric into piles with an average of seven to eight different fabrics to create one dress. I created an empire waist style dress with varying lengths on the sleeves, drop waist dresses, skirts, jumpers, vests, all very slimming and flattering. The dresses ranged in sizes from two to twenty eight. Friends began bringing me their old clothes, fabric pieces, buttons and vintage laces.

I hired my next door neighbor to help me as I took over one of the bedrooms in our house as my studio. The energy was divine. The fabrics began to take on a life of their own. In the mornings when I went into my studio, as if by magic, I would see color combinations that I hadn't thought of, as the fabrics seemed to come alive. I was completely inspired and consumed with creative energy. We created two dozen dresses that were well received at the art show. What I hadn't sold that day, I took to my friend's Garden and Gift store. She was thrilled to carry them in her store. I brought her six dresses that sold right away. She was selling them almost as fast as I could make them.

Each dress took eight hours to make and weighed the same as four dresses put together. I went to store owners, showing them my dresses, hoping that they would purchase them. I was very nervous and anxious as they judged my work. I was accepted by an exclusive clothing store, but my low self-esteem issues got in the way. I panicked. I was unable to follow through on such a great offer, so I decided to open my own store. I found a great old brick storefront downtown with a beautiful picture window, a cute Dutch door, and private bathroom. I wrote the landlord a check for the first and last month's rent, and then prayed that he didn't cash it until Ralph's check came in. At the time, the rent on the store was more than our mortgage. I purchased second hand glass display cases to use as counter space. I brought in a Franklin stove and added a rocking chair for ambiance. My father-in-law built a dressing room that I decoupaged with fabrics pieces. My sewing partner's step-dad gave me a great deal on some rose colored carpeting. Ralph helped me set up my work stations so that I could create and sew while I was standing up. A girlfriend designed a cute logo that I used on my business cards and clothing tags as well as the sign in the window.

Ralph brought home a huge wooden spool end from a cable spool and on it we painted and stenciled my store's name and address. The city sign approvers didn't like that it was a round sign instead of the standard rectangle until a woman on their staff pointed out that it represented a spool of thread. I had not even noticed the significance of the spool in relationship to the type of store I had. She was an angel for noticing and the sign was approved. I was turning forty and, coincidently, the address of my business was forty. Ralph installed overhead lighting. I purchased antique dress forms from thrift stores, found a wicker love seat that I placed out front, surrounded by potted plants. And I began sewing like a crazy lady. My neighbor/sewing partner had a sister-in-law from Mexico who lived near us who had her own sewing machine. In the past she had sewn clothing for a large company in Mexico. After I pinned all the fabrics together to make pattern pieces, she would then top stitch all the pieces and clip the inside seams. I opened the store with two dozen dresses, which I immediately sold. I soon realized that I needed to get serious about this new venture, so we got to work creating enough inventory to keep the store full.

It was interesting to find that the customers always seemed to want the dress that I was currently working on, which kept me motivated and inspired. Word got out that I had opened up a unique clothing store and, before long; I was approached by the local edition of the LA Times. They wanted to do a feature on me and my store for their lifestyle section. They did a wonderful job and I received a lot of positive attention from the public. Shortly after that the local county newspaper also did a feature on me and my store. I could feel my life changing for the better; now I no longer felt like a helpless victim. I was able to set up my work station to accommodate my injured back, let the wonderful magical creativity flow as I created beautiful works of art that people were delighted to own.

In the beginning, the act of putting myself out there was very uncomfortable, but it was the perfect way to develop confidence and raise my level of self-esteem. It was giving me great joy helping to make others feel good about themselves and their bodies. Ralph suggested that I include my story, how I came to be making these creations, on the price tags that I had created. In the beginning, I was against it thinking that people did not want to hear my story. Then, as people began reading my story, it resulted in us making a heart connection. It was an inspiring story and many people could relate, feeling inspired and hopeful. I am very thankful for Ralph's suggestion. I have since learned that I and others can help each other as we are all connected in some way and have very similar experiences.

I became friends with the other women shop owners, where we shared experiences and advice with each other. It was wonderful connecting with the other women as we supported each other; they began to feel like family to me. I also became interested in the local political scene. I realized that the local officials' main focus was on the businesses downtown and that what they decided had a direct effect on me as well as other business owners. I became a part of the business community, participating in the holiday art walks. I enjoyed decorating my store for the holidays, creating a positive relationship with my town and its people.

I had my store for four years and I enjoyed meeting people and making them happy. Once my lease was up, I decided that I would like to reach a much bigger audience. The local county fair ran for eleven days every year and it was visited by tens of thousands of people every day. I spent months sewing, with the help of two other women, to create enough of an inventory for the event. I was enjoying being at home without interruption as I furiously created. We had moved to a larger house and I had a huge sun-filled studio where I was surrounded by beautiful fabrics. During that time, inspiration would sometimes wake me up at 3:00 am to work on yet another creation.

During those eleven days, I was at my booth twelve hours a day. The artisans' booths were in a large tent with dirt floors and portable toilets but we artists made it feel special. We became a community helping each other out. It was amazing how many people came through our tent. At night, it was cold with the ocean breeze and I sold so many baby hats that I brought my sewing machine to my booth to keep up with the demand. The booth space rent was very reasonable and we had lots of time to set up and tear down. I sold a lot of items and I enjoyed the fair atmosphere. Several people approached me, wanting me to be a vendor at their functions. I attended several small shows until I joined the Harvest Festival, an artisans' seasonal show which travels around California featuring high-end arts, crafts and food items. It had a wonderful feel to it that attracted the cliental that would appreciate my clothing.

We purchased a motorhome and travelled with it packed to the ceiling with all the items needed to set up my booth. Most of the Harvest Festival locations were at fairgrounds that had great facilities for parking our motorhome. There were over two dozen of us who travelled this way. The requirements for our booth were very strict and regulated. We had to bring our own lighting, flooring, canopy, walls, tables, chairs that all had to be preapproved and fitting within the country theme of long ago.

We would arrive on a Thursday to set our booth up. These were big events and there were a lot of vehicles with people vying for space. Every show had a different floor plan so you never knew where you would be setting up or which building you would be in until you arrived. It was mayhem trying to get everything finished in one day, or less, if we arrived late due to vehicle problems, traffic, or the dreaded "lost" situations. Driving the large motorhome through big cities was harrowing at best. By choice I am the driver in our family and it was stressful for me going through large busy cities. It was additionally stressful for Ralph to be my navigator, but we always made it. We worked hard setting everything up. We brought our bicycles with us and, when we finished setting up, we would ride into town for dinner and a movie.

We made friends with other vendors who were also camping out. We would gather together in the evenings telling stories of our worst and best shows and our biggest mistakes we made with our motorhomes, which mostly involved driving away while the drain pipes were still hooked up to the dump stations. Most shows were a week apart, so we had free time in-between to relax or travel around sightseeing.

154

On Sunday late afternoon, we would begin tearing down our booth so that we were packed and ready to be on the road before the sun went down. It became a contest amongst the many vendors to see who could tear down the fastest. It was exhausting hard work but the show-times were a lot of fun with music, entertainment, art, crafts, and lots of trading going on. I acquired some very beautiful jewelry, art, music, food, etc. It was a world all its own, where we all enjoyed creating an atmosphere that our customers enjoyed. I never did seem to have enough stock on hand, as my two helpers and I couldn't sew fast enough. My creations were one of a kind and I needed to carry a large range of sizes. The booth rent was very high but, if I booked a certain number of shows, the rate was slightly reduced and the booth fees were paid six months in advance. The shows were held in the fall through to Christmas. After four years, we were able to determine what shows were best for us and planned accordingly. Ralph was able to take off work during the shows and we enjoyed our time together. The women customers really liked having Ralph there with me, as he has a delightful personality and made them feel at ease.

Then the 9-11 tragedy happened, which changed everything. We had a show scheduled four days later. The mood was heavy, as most of us were glued to the radio listening to what was happening. The show producers insisted that no radios be playing during the show and that we were to always keep those smiles on our faces. Some of the vendors' skin color or clothing displeased the customers, causing stress for us all. The news media advised the general public to avoid large venues as well as large gathering places such as fair-grounds and malls, all places where

155

our shows were being held. Attendance dropped to nearly nothing. Inside a Harvest Festival, the world is different by design where we were to create a theme of a time long past, disconnected from the current world. Now we were sober and scared. The promoters offered no refunds on our booth fees and, if we continued, we would only lose more money.

I decided, after doing this art for ten years, I was ready to put it down. My body was tired and in need of a rest from all the physical demands. I am so glad that I discovered this creative ability within me and by my ability to express it while sharing it with others. I didn't make much money, most artists don't, yet I have no regrets. It was a wonderful time in my life. It brought me out of my suicidal depression and made me feel good about myself. I still get emails from friends saying that they had seen someone walking around town wearing one of my lovely creations.

SOULTHRIVER

CHAPTER EIGHT

I was very fortunate to begin my healing process in the 1980's when self-help was up and coming. I also was very lucky to live in a town that provided numerous modalities towards the healing process. I tried as many things as I could and each one assisted me in the process of my peeling away at the onion. Layer after layer was shed, mostly painful, foul and tear filled. I can't say that there was one thing that cured me, as each thing I tried brought me closer and closer to being healed. The bookstores now had whole sections labeled Self-Help. There were specials on Public Television and articles in the local newspapers. Often the local government office buildings provided space for ACA (Adult Children of Alcoholics) meetings during the day, before and after work. I poured all my energy into healing, as I desperately wanted to stay alive. It is amazing how my life went way beyond my wildest dreams. Not only did I stay alive, I thrived. I have experienced wondrous healings that I never dreamt possible. There were profound changes happening in my life that seemed to happen all on their own. The rewards for doing the work are never-ending.

Survivor of Incest Anonymous (SIA) Group has a beautiful one page document called "The Promises." I am here to tell you that they come true. Because of the sexual abuse I experienced, I was deeply, deeply jealous. My first husband gave me reasons to be jealous from the day we married. But jealously did not leave me when we divorced. My jealousy reared its ugly head when Ralph and I became a couple. It was uncontrollable, unrealistic and unfounded. If he was out of my sight I was certain he was having sex with some other girl, even if it was one isle away in the supermarket. We lived five minutes from the beach, where we loved to go boogey boarding and it was torture for me seeing women walking around in their bathing suits. It was almost more than I could stand. When I look at pictures of me during that time, it is only now that I realize how pretty I was and had nothing to worry about. Ralph was a loving and faithful husband, but I was not reacting realistically. These reactions were purely emotional and not based in reality. To appease me, we went to the beaches that were hard to get to, isolated, and dangerous.

I hated it when Ralph would be talking to our women neighbors, even though they were my friends. I was constantly having nightmares where he was having sex with some other woman. When I awoke, I was very angry with him. At his job, he dealt mostly with women as he managed their office buildings. Often he would receive calls at home from these women and that pushed more of my red-hot buttons. He had frequent lunch dates with women that caused my imagination to go to the darkest place possible. This was putting a strain on our marriage.

I was unable to watch sex scenes on television or at the movies without being extremely triggered. We were watching a very popular movie on television when I freaked out at the beginning of a sex scene. I ran outside and began punching the cushions of our outdoor patio chaise lounge until my fists bled. My body seemed to need a physical outlet for these emotions, as I felt as though I would implode. After that, we bought a punching bag and my brother-in-law taught me how to put on the gloves by myself so I could use the bag whenever I felt the need. Ralph hung the bag and, with chalk, he drew a picture of my father on it. As I punched away, the image would slowly disappear as would the anger, panic and anxiety. I thought these reactions within me were a permanent broken part of me that would never heal, that this was part of the damage I had received, and I would need to accept it and keep it under control.

Years into my recovery, Ralph and I were walking down the street as a strikingly beautiful young woman was walking towards us. I casually mentioned to Ralph how beautiful she was. That is when I noticed that something in me had changed. I no longer felt shrouded by the green monster that controlled my reactions to what I perceived as sexual situations. I had developed a healthy and natural reaction to beauty, sensuality, and sexuality. This was amazing in that it was never a goal I worked towards. I had seen my jealousy and fear of sexuality as a defect that I had no control over; now I found that I was healing from that ugliness. This was just one of the many benefits I received from doing the work of recovery. I had immersed myself in this process just to keep alive but now miracles were happening within me, and they still are.

The Universe generously assisted in keeping me from undermining my progress. One recurring theme was the guilt I had around divorcing my parents. I felt shame and guilt about making them the "bad guys." I told myself that maybe I was exaggerating the effects of the abuse or I was blowing things out of proportion. Scenarios played in my head on how maybe we could reunite, but every time I decided to act on these fantasies, word would get back to me about something horrible my parents had done, putting an end to that fantasy. I struggled with the guilt relative to the pain that I imagined I was causing my parents. It was becoming evident that I had internalized their pain and guilt.

A wonderful therapist described forgiveness in such a way that I could accept it, as he stated that forgiveness is giving back the problem, disease and pain to whom it belongs, for this was not something I needed to carry inside me any longer. As the saying goes: "I didn't Cause it, I can't Control it, and I can't Cure it." The damage inflicted on me is not mine and it belongs back onto the owners. It is about removing that which I do not deserve; therefore, no interaction is required, and no guilt is involved. This was no longer my shit that I wore around my neck choking the life out of me. This was an ugliness that was injected into me, running through my veins, changing me down to my very DNA to make me hate myself, challenging my very existence. But it didn't kill me. It has given me such a perspective on life as to what is now important and what is not. I am becoming the finest tempered sword that is bettered and stronger from having been thrust into the fires.

As I walked the path of recovery, I frequently would stop to take a personal inventory of myself. I had noticed that I was still carrying my smart-ass, know-it-all attitude that I had developed as a child in order to keep people away from me. I observed myself in conversations with others, noticing how I constantly interjected, taking control of the conversation, and all the while flaunting my self-absorbed self. In order to rein myself in, I consciously and literally bit my tongue to allow the conversation to continue without my input. I would then observe if what I would have said would have added anything of importance to the conversation. The more I practiced, the calmer I became. I started learning how to listen and, the more I practiced this restraint, the more my intuition came through. I now listen to my intuition while holding my tongue and many times I found that what I would have said in the past was either not appropriate or not what the person needed to hear. More and more I believed that everyone and everything in my life is there for a reason and I can learn from my surroundings if I stay calm and centered.

During one of my therapy group sessions, one of the women turned to me and told me that I whine when I talk and I heard her. I immediately began listening to myself and was able to remove the whiny tone from my voice. I realized that I have the ability to change. I can change my reactions, beliefs, thoughts, feelings and words. I survived some pretty horrible shit in my life and I owe it to myself to be my first priority and become the best I can and to share my experience, strength and hope. I don't really have heroes or gurus in my life as I believe that we can become our own heroes. We all have paths to follow on this journey and I am dedicated to following mine.

In the past, I had a saying that the effects of the sexual abuse on me was as if my hand had been cut off and that I would never be whole or regrow another one but I could still function and adapt. Now I believe that I am whole, no longer do I feel disabled by the abuse. What I have experienced is my story and it is what makes me who I am and how I came to be this person.

I had suffered two physical manifestations due to the incest. One was chronic vaginal yeast infections, which I had from a young age. It was very painful, itchy, and burning, making it very hard to sit in class. When my mother discovered that I had an infection, she called her gynecologist who said she couldn't see me as I had not yet started my periods and she considered me too young for a pelvic exam. After suffering years with these infections, her doctor finally agreed to see me and I was diagnosed with yeast infections. I don't remember anything being prescribed using anything topical to help deal with this. In high school it got worse as I sat through class in agony with no relief.

The other physical manifestation was a large red mark on the side of my neck about the size of a silver dollar. The mark showed up the day my father raped me. Whenever I became nervous or stressed the mark would turn a bright red. My mother used it as a gauge to see if I was lying to her or had done something wrong. She did not know the origin of the mark but used it to her advantage. A doctor burned it with dry ice causing a large water blister and told me that, when the blister popped, the mark might be gone, but it wasn't.

These physical manifestations were making it harder and harder for me to ignore what was happening to me on the outside as well as the inside of me. Over the course of many years of therapy, the yeast infections became less and less and the red mark became duller and duller until they both finally disappeared.

In the beginning era of my therapy, there was one particularly bad day where I was feeling the need to release pent up negative feelings within my body, so I beat on my pillow until I over exerted myself, managing to pull a muscle in my back. It was very painful so I went to my family physician and he recommended that I see a massage therapist. I had never had a massage and wasn't sure that I was comfortable with being touched and I positively knew I couldn't see a man. I had several friends who were receiving massages from a local woman and they highly recommended her. I made an appointment with her. I was very nervous but I knew this was something that was important for me to do for myself. The massage turned out to be very wonderful and healing. My body was responding to the healthy touch. I have since enjoyed hundreds of massages and continue to get massages as a way to take care of myself and to reward myself for all the hard work I have done.

Other things I have done to take care of myself are through Tai Chi, Chi Gong, Yoga, Meditation, walking, and being in nature. All of these soothe me and bring me great comfort in the low times or just when I need to be uplifted.

SOULTHRIVER

CHAPTER NINE

For over twenty years, I have participated in a yearly, three-day-long, Women's Retreat that was put on by those of us in my women's group. One year when I arrived home from enjoying one of these retreats, Ralph informed me that he had smoked pot with a friend of ours while I was gone. Up until then, Ralph had been clean and sober for over fifteen years. I was not sure of the repercussions this new event would present. He had relapsed and I was not sure how to handle this. At first, things appeared to be under control, and then he slowly started to act totally out of character. He was not acting like he had in the past when he smoked pot. He said that the pot was making him paranoid but I had never seen him being affected this way. Pot had always made him so mellow. I was confused at the change in his personality. I began to worry. We were in the middle of renovating our home and he was unable to stay in the house for more than fifteen minutes at a time without rushing back to his garage, not returning for hours.

He began staying up all night, going to work in the morning. One late night when he was working on something in the garage, he shot a nail through his index finger. When he went to the doctor the next day, the doctor put him on disability for the next two months. I never saw Ralph so excited over anything else before; you would have thought he had won the lottery. In fact, I told him that he was happier with that news than the day we got married. With him home all day, things began to get worse. He had caught our stove on fire and dealt with it by pulling the top off and lowering it down from the third story balcony. One morning before sunrise, he created an explosion in the garage and denied doing it.

I was a mess. This was not the behavior of a pot smoker. I didn't know what was happening to my husband of over twenty-two years. The stress began to take a toll on me, though I didn't see the connection at that time. I did not know what was happening to my husband and I was in intense emotional pain. Everything out of Ralph's mouth was a lie. He was quickly losing weight and looking horrible. I began having bowel problems. I was having explosive diarrhea. I was unable to finish a meal without having to run downstairs to the bathroom. Most times I was unable to reach the toilet in time. I would then have to strip off my clothes and take a shower. Everything was running violently through my body, and I was rapidly losing weight. I was experiencing intense gnawing in my stomach as if I hadn't eaten in weeks.

I was employed as a gardener and, when I squatted down, my bowels would release a horrible smelly, dark coffee-ground-like diarrhea and I would have to rush home. Frequently, I would suddenly realize that my underwear was full of this excrement even though I hadn't felt a thing happening. I did not understand what was happening to me and I became fearful. My doctor referred me to a gastroenterologist who ran blood test, stool samples, colonoscopies, barium enemas, upper GI's, lower GI's until he concluded that, in his opinion, I was suffering from a rare pancreatic cancer. He had ordered tests to confirm his suspicions, and then left for a vacation out of the country for a month. My return visit was for one month later to go over the test results. That was the longest month of my life.

I researched this disease and discovered that what the doctor suspected was a rare form of cancer that rapidly progressed throughout the body with only a 20% chance of survival. Ralph and I went into emergency mode. We talked of him quitting his job and asking his father for money so we could travel around the world trying to enjoy ourselves before I died.

As I was getting sicker, Ralph's behavior was getting more and more bizarre. Things started to make sense when I found a vial of cocaine in his bathroom and I confronted him with this find. He threw the vial away and declared that he would not do it again. A couple of days later, I saw him snorting cocaine in his car as he was leaving for work. I then told him that he was killing my best friend, him, and that I could not be dealing with fighting cancer while he was doing drugs, that he would need to leave. I was devastated with his relapse and my illness.

I was driving to the doctor's office one day when I noticed that the New Age music playing on my radio was irritating me. I was numb and wanted to feel something, so I found a heavy metal radio station and turned the radio full blast. I enjoyed feeling the screaming and sarcasm yelling at me through the radio. The pounding bass filled my veins with anger and despair and I began to feel suicidal. I believed that if I was to slit my wrists, all of these bad feelings would drain out of me. I wanted to experience what that would feel like. I even thought of punishing Ralph by starting smoking cigarettes once again. It was becoming obvious to me that I desperately needed help. One week later we went to the doctor for the test results and were told that I did not have cancer. The doctor concluded the appointment with stating that "Sometimes these problems are just from what we eat" then sent me home.

After that I decided not to return to his office again. When Ralph found out that I wasn't dying, he reacted poorly. He was not happy that he no longer had my illness as an excuse to get high.

My therapist at the time told me that I should see my doctor about taking anti-anxiety medication. In my weakened condition I was enjoying the lethargy I was experiencing in my body. It was the first time that I could remember not feeling anxious. I realized that anxiety had been a constant state of being for me. I saw my doctor, told her what was going on in my life, and she prescribed an anti-anxiety medication that was gentle and non-addicting. The medication allowed me to be present during an anxiety inducing situation so I no longer went out of control. I no longer wanted to jump in my car and drive like a madwoman when I was faced with a stressful situation. My reactions began to not be completely physically driven.

I started using my intuition, higher self and the Universe to problem solve. I was using my adult-self to work through crisis instead of allowing my inner-child to be in control. Choosing to take medication or not is a very personal choice. I believe that for the short term, it is very helpful and, for some, lifesaving. It was not explained to me that it was a short-term tool to be used towards helping me claim my authentic, intuitive, spiritual self. I took the medication for ten years, afraid that I would lose all that I had gained through "modern medicine." Little did I realize that, once I became centered and self-confident, I was capable of making great strides in my growth without the medication. I had been relying on the medication instead of on myself. I am grateful for the assistance it provided. I wish now that, for ten years, I hadn't depended on it instead of myself.

I began going to a friend who had just become an acupuncturist. When I told her of my symptoms she said that it sounded like I was allergic to gluten. I then went to my doctor where I was tested and diagnosed with Celiac disease. Once I learned the symptoms of this disease, I realized that I had had the disease my entire life and that the stress I had been experiencing had exacerbated it to the point of being life threatening. Celiac disease not only affected my physical health, it also affected my mental health. Some of my most bizarre thinking can be traced to the gluten I had consumed. I believe that my father also suffers from Celiac disease, which can explain some of the physical, mental and emotional problems he has had in his life.

Even though I was diagnosed with this disease, it took several years before I became pro-active with my health by trying to eliminate gluten from my diet and health care products. I found that, even though I knew the cookie in my hand that I was going to eat would make me sick and likely to cause disturbance in my personality, I ate it anyway. I found myself once again punishing myself through my diet. I was no different than a drug or alcohol abuser. Gluten was bad for me and while I would greatly regret consuming it, I felt out of control. There is no 12-step group for this disease yet. I needed one so I applied everything I had learned from the many 12-step meetings I had attended to slowly regain control over what I ingested. I then learned to stop punishing myself once again for being who I am.

Two months later, Ralph went back to work and my therapist recommended that I start attending Al-Anon meetings. I walked into my first meeting completely at my wits ends. I wanted help on how I could get my husband to stop doing drugs. I was shocked to see three of my best girlfriends sitting at the table. Surely they could tell me how to get Ralph clean and sober. I was an emotional wreck and was so overwhelmed with despair that I didn't hear a word of the opening literature being read. As I calmed down, I heard men and women tell how happy they were to have an addict/alcoholic in their lives. All I could think was "What a bunch of fucking idiots." They didn't know what my life was like or what I was living with. I was disgusted that they were happy. All I wanted was for them to give me the book of instructions telling me how to get my husband sober and to stay that way. Where was the magic spell I could place on him?

Then I heard them speak. One at a time, over and over again, they shared their experience, strength and hope. I heard my story flowing out of the mouths of others. I took home a newcomer's packet that was filled with helpful information. I hid the pamphlets in my dresser drawer, pulling them out to read after Ralph had gone to work. I bought and read everything I could. They had a wonderful book on surviving a marriage with an addict. I attended three, sometimes four, meetings a week. I began to truly listen to these people tell their stories. I had my three girlfriends acting as my sponsor. When I was low, I would call them, telling them how bad Ralph was being and they would gently remind me that it was all about me, not him. Slowly I learned that I needed to take my focus off Ralph and place it on me.

I had to look at what it was about me that liked the trauma, drama and abuse? Why did I occupy all my time focusing on Ralph with his addiction instead of me and my well-being? As I turned my focus inwards, looking at myself, I became a grateful member of Al-Anon. Even though Ralph and I were suffering, we also realized how much we loved each other and wanted to be well. Through the meetings I began to blossom and this started to have a positive effect on our home life and marriage. Ralph had decided to start rehab on his birthday. One month prior to his birthday, he chose to join an intensive outpatient drug rehab program. There we received individual and family counseling, followed by weekly family and friends informational workshops where we received an intense education on the issues of drug abuse and addiction.

Slowly we began to heal the devastation of what two years of relapse had had on our psyches, our bodies as well as our relationship. We soon had dozens of friends from AA, NA and Al-Anon. We attended 12-step campouts, workshops and get-togethers. I was even asked to lead SIA meetings at some of these functions. I was now a proud member of those "fucking idiots" who embraces the addicts in our lives, myself included. I have come to learn that I, too, am an addict; smoking, drinking and drugging and also addicted to my co-dependency. I was using someone else, Ralph, to focus on in order to avoid dealing with the real issue, ME!!!!

I believe that Ralph's relapse and recovery took us to a higher level. We learned a deeper understanding and a broader knowledge of what was truly important to us. This work is not for sissies as we pulled ourselves inside out. We dove down to the deepest darkest places within ourselves and it wasn't pretty. We fought, we blamed, and we accused each other. Trust had been lost and needed to be regained. We were nearing our twenty-fifth wedding anniversary and wondered if it was worth all that we were going through. As we slowly stopped blaming each other, we started to take responsibility for our own actions and life began to change. The clouds began to lift and we began to plan and put into action those things that would make us happy.

As I grew stronger, my focus on being a victim lessened and lessened. I began to connect with the spirit within me that had originally sought a human experience. My spirit had not been crushed or killed by my experiences as these experiences were making me stronger. I was learning to tell my story and the importance of being able to listen to the stories of others. In my determination to heal from my secrets, I told it all. Our meeting rooms would be figuratively covered in terror, vomit, excrement, blood, death, violations, ritual abuse, rapes, abortions, self-inflicted wounds, bestiality, mutilations and more. This was where true healing began. As the saying goes, we are only as sick as our secrets.

I attended SIA meetings faithfully as if my life depended on it, because I believed it did. There was an unfortunate period where events drastically affected SIA meetings and attendance. There was a false memory movement that had officials, along with therapists, believe that the abuse memories were after-planted memories, not genuine, so they could not be believed. This greatly affected the victims of sexual abuse. Victims' stories were being challenged, and accusers of abuse could be charged legally by the accused. This was a terrible blow to the healing process of untold numbers of survivors, resulting in the survivors becoming the bad guys. There were huge consequences for accusing the abuser, as the abusers had the protection of the law. The abusing priests had the protection of the church. There were therapists willing to back up the false memory syndrome. It became dangerous to tell our stories with the threat that we could be taken to court and sued.

173

Consequently, meeting attendance dropped considerably; we no longer felt safe advertising our meetings. We became fearful that some attendees may have ulterior motives. We no longer wanted to share about our abuse with our family, friends or newcomers. Outreach efforts were rarely seen.

When Ralph had his drug relapse, meetings became our first priority. After several years of AA, NA and Al Anon, we wanted SIA meetings back into our lives. Years later, when meetings did resurface, they were scarce and too often had deviated from the original 12-step program. Some meetings now were being led by those who called themselves facilitators, controlling the meetings. Ralph and I joined one such meeting, hoping to regain what we had in the past. We felt that the group lacked integrity along with personal ownership, so we started a true 12-step SIA meeting based on the 12-steps of AA.

In the beginnings of SIA, the only way to locate a meeting was to request a meeting directory to be mailed to you. When computers became popular, an email containing a directory was sent out. Now there is a directory posted on their website with instant access to meetings locations. This is incredibly helpful to those who are in desperate need of a meeting. Most of us seek a meeting at our lowest point or are directed by our therapist to find a meeting.

We started up a new SIA meeting in town and I registered my first name and phone number as a contact person for that area on the SIA directory. I received on average one or two calls a week. Most of these calls came from people who had never told anyone about the abuse they suffered. I learned how to be a good listener and encouraged them to attend a meeting. Such a small percent of survivors reach out for help with an even smaller percentage taking that first step. I am a true believer in SIA. I have seen miracles happen with peoples' lives. It is hard work, no.... it is Fucking Hard Work!!!

SOULTHRIVER

176

CHAPTER TEN

Six years after our sister reunion, we were reunited once again when Lynn was on one of her yearly visits. Lynn now was two years sober and Jean was working on her sobriety. Jean and Ruth were both living with our parents. Sean had built himself a house on my parents' land and they all spent a lot of time together. Sean's one true love is motorcycle riding, so he and my father purchased enough motorcycles so that Sean and my sisters could all ride together. For a year, unbeknownst to me, they had been visiting a riding area near our house. Sean called one day to say that he, along with my sisters, would all be riding there if we would like to join them. I was thrilled but apprehensive. I needed to take this opportunity that once again the Universe was providing me, yet I knew I might get my feelings hurt in the process.

Growing up, we spent many vacations camping in the desert and riding motorcycles. Our family only had one bike that we kids could share and we never had the chance to ride together. I always managed to get into some kind of trouble when I was riding. There was something about the freedom, the speed and the vast space. I spent a lot of time being grounded for riding too fast or being gone too long, but it was worth it. As much as I loved riding, I started to relate it to being in trouble. I felt as though I was a bad person and I eventually no longer enjoyed riding. I decided I was going to join my sisters and Sean, but I had also decided I wouldn't ride. We arrived just as they were finishing up riding and everything was being loaded up. We had brought some food and we all sat around eating lunch and catching each other up on our lives. I was so happy I went to see them. Lynn left the next day.

A year later when Lynn was back for another visit, Sean called to tell me that they had been riding for the last week; tomorrow was to be their last day, and would we like to join them? Years earlier, I had overcome my aversion to riding and Ralph and I now owned quads that we rode around on our property. We took our riding gear with us and joined them. Our quads at home were automatics and it had been decades since I used a clutch. I needed help and my sisters gladly took me under their wings. Ruth rode in front of me while Jean rode behind. Ruth motioned to me when I needed to shift up or down while Jean was there, in case I fell. This was the very first time I allowed them to take care of me. I willingly found myself giving them my full trust. I was a little shaky at first as we climbed mountains, dodged rocks, and hugged curves. As I became more comfortable with the bike and trusting in their experience, the riding began to feel so loving, healthy and right. This was so unlike our childhood dynamic. We had so much fun as we whooped and hollered. We were quite a sight with our helmets, boots, chest guards, gloves, goggles and shin guards. We were grandmothers feeling like teenagers again. It was a magical feeling to receive their patient care, love, and understanding. Tears poured down my face. I dearly love my sisters and this was the best experience I had ever had with them. The next day, I was sore and bruised but I felt a great healing had taken place. I will never forget that day.

SOULTHRIVER

CHAPTER ELEVEN

Throughout my life, I have become aware of certain talents within me. I was maybe twelve or thirteen when I realized that I had a certain unusual talent. I discovered this one afternoon as a group of us kids were hanging around the end of our street. We were all sitting on the curb and one of the boys pulled out a penny and challenged the rest of us to guess if it was heads or tails after he flipped it in the air. After each flip I closed my eyes and concentrated, took a deep breath, then in my mind's-eye I could see the penny. I guessed correctly ten out of ten flips.

About this time I also realized that, if I stared at the back of someone's neck, I could get him or her to turn around. As my friends and I rode in the back of the school bus, they would pick out someone sitting ahead of us, then challenge me to get them to turn around and I was successful every time. This was particularly fun with the cute boys, getting them to turn around and notice us. I then found that if I thought of someone, shortly afterwards, they would either call me or show up at my door. When playing the game of picking a number, I could usually guess the correct number. I thoroughly enjoyed these talents that made me feel unique and powerful.

I have found that my personal energy field somehow prevents me from wearing a watch for very long before it quits working. Same thing with flashlights; no matter how fresh the battery, they will lose their illuminating power when I hold them. Ralph usually refuses to let me hold the flashlights, especially the ones with very expensive batteries.

I had extensive dental work done as a young adult, including several cavities filled and a dozen root canals with crowns. When I experienced pain in my mouth, it was difficult for me to determine which tooth was bothering me as the pain would radiate throughout my mouth. My dentist had just learned a new technique at UCLA called Muscle Testing. He would have me raise my arm straight out from my side as he placed a finger on one of my teeth, while putting his other hand on top of my extended wrist. He would then gently place pressure to my wrist; if I was able to resist and keep my arm level it meant that that tooth was not the problem. When he reached the problem tooth, I was unable to keep my arm perpendicular, no matter how hard I tried.

Years later, once again, I had a toothache but could not determine, by using my tongue, which tooth was causing the pain. I was in my car on my way to work, stopped at a stop sign. I stuck my finger in my mouth to see if I could feel which tooth was aching. As I touched the culprit, the engine in my car slowed way down. As I removed my finger, it sped back up to its normal rpm's. I touched that tooth again, and again the car slowed way down. Now I knew what tooth needed attention.

I took a Physic Awareness class at the local college and, in that class, I told the instructor about these experiences. She told me that I needed to practice these talents. So the next weekend, as Ralph and I lay in bed, I looked out our sliding glass door to our greenhouse where I saw the turbines on the roof spinning to release the built- up warm air from inside. As the two turbines spun, I concentrated on one of the turbines with the intention of getting it to stop and, sure enough, that turbine did stop as the other one continued to spin and spin. Ralph and I thought this was pretty cool. The next morning as we lay in bed, I looked up at the ceiling fan that was spinning like an airplane propeller. I once again focused on the blades where, luckily, Ralph saw what I was doing and told me to stop. He pointed out that I could possibly burn up the motor.

When I had injured my back, there was some nerve damage to my left leg and I needed to have tests done to see how extensive the damage was. I was tested twice on an EMG machine that sent electrical shocks through my skin to the nerve and then its course of travel was recorded. One of the machines was ancient looking and as the test was being performed, it somehow picked up the radio waves of the local Spanish radio station. The doctor was as surprised as I was and said this had never happened before. After one of these tests, I had a massage appointment. As I lay on the massage table, the massage therapist went to touch me and received electrical shocks coming from my body. This lasted for ten minutes, before all the electricity was eliminated from my body.

During the time in which I was in psychotherapy, I would frequently be overcome with dizziness and nausea and I had assumed it was a side effect of the therapy. Over time, it included feeling the floor shake. On one occasion, I was in night school class when I began feeling a pretty big earthquake. As I looked around the classroom I realized that no one else seemed to be feeling it. I then looked at the hanging items but noticed that they were not moving at all, yet I was certain I had just felt a pretty good earthquake. The next day in the news, there was a report of a very strong earthquake in China. I thought this had to be more than a coincidence, yet I told no one. These experiences started happening on a more frequent basis. I found out that there was an earthquake somewhere in the world the same time I was feeling it. Sometimes after I sensed a large tremor, I would become overwhelmed with grief and despair. On those occasions, the earthquakes were responsible for large numbers of deaths and destruction. I did not like predicting anyone's death, so in the beginning, I was very uncomfortable with this ability. I didn't like keeping these feelings to myself, so I started telling Ralph when I felt an earthquake. I now had someone who validated my experience. One of my wise crone friends called this sensitivity as "Being in touch with the collective consciousness." Feeling collective energy made this easier for me to accept.

I am also more sensitive to the small local earthquakes that frequent Southern California. There is a website that records earthquakes and asks people to post their experiences with any recent events. When I would feel an earthquake that seemed to be local, I would look at that site and found that it had registered and I began to add my local experience to the site. I then searched for information about the ability to predict earthquakes and found that the majority of the population involved with monitoring and recording earthquakes claimed that it was impossible to predict earthquakes, so I decided to not report my predictions.

My psychic awareness instructor believes that everyone has psychic abilities, while some are more developed than others. I believe that I have developed mine because of the abuse I was suffering as a child. It feels like a power all mine; no one can take that away from me.

There is some small part of me that remembers being a spirit before I was born and my developed talent feels like a part of my prior existence. Deep down inside, I feel that I brought with me a sense of security and that is what helped me stay alive.

There are people who believe that we pick our parents for the learning experience they will provide. I once had a psychic palm reader tell me that the parents I had picked were not ready for me, so I wound up with the ones I have. Part of that resonates with me knowing how impatient, insistent and goal-driven I am. I can just see me whining, "I am ready, and I want to go now!" But I am now learning that my heritage is exactly what I needed so that I could learn to be the person I have now become.

While I was married to Jack, he went through a religious phase where he was a very churchy guy on the outside, even at times carrying a bible around. He placed Jesus stickers on my car, though not on his. When we first married, he was a member of the Mormon Church. While in England, we attended a Mormon church on Base and he belonged to a church men's group. I'm not sure what he did to cause it but, after a couple of months, we were excommunicated from the church and were no longer allowed to attend church services.

After that, Jack found a group that was referred to by others as "Jesus Freaks." The group was led by a couple that was ten years older than the rest of us. They used the Living Bible and called themselves "Disciples of Jesus." They were actually very sweet, kind and loving people who had gatherings once a week at their house where we had prayer circles and lively discussions. Little did I know that Jack was using the group to find girlfriends to preach his special message to and, once his secret was discovered, the wife of the couple told me that I should divorce him.

One church that the group of us attended was located in the English countryside; the preacher was a woman, and everyone came to Sunday services dressed in their everyday clothes. The church was packed with local and military folks. Every Sunday, the preacher would ask for people to come to the altar to receive the Holy Spirit. On one Sunday I felt drawn to go to the front of the church to receive this gift, though not as what they represented it. Their experience and use of this gift was what people call "Holy Rollers" rolling on the ground; eyes rolled back, body jerking and speaking in a crazy language. After going to the altar and "accepting the Holy Spirit" I found that, when I was praying, I was speaking in "tongues," a language totally unfamiliar to me.

I felt compelled to speak this foreign language nearly every night as I tried to fall asleep. I soon noticed I was sobbing and had the feeling that I was praying for a woman far away, that I was grieving for her suffering as I sobbed.

Years later, I spent my work lunch breaks taking long walks along the small flight line that was located at the end of our office building. The airstrip was situated between vast areas of produce fields that were very peaceful. There were lots of birds and the area was surrounded by blue skies and gently sloping hills. As I walked, I would weep and pray in this strange language. On nights that I couldn't sleep, I would speak this language in my head until I fell asleep. In my imagination, this was a very personal act between me, this woman and God. It was very comforting for me as it helped me to release tension, anxiety and sadness.

Over a period of more than twenty years of praying this way, I realized that the woman I grieved and sobbed for was actually ME. In my imagination, this woman was someone far

185

removed and outside of myself. I saw her as having dark skin and sad eyes. She felt hopeless and all alone as we prayed to God asking that she be helped. I believe that the Universe disguised this gift to protect me from the truth that I was not yet prepared to face and a way to release the pressure and turmoil from my boiling insides. I believe that it was much easier for me to feel compassion and love for a stranger than I could feel for myself, and it worked.

Creating Soul Cards has been a very powerful healing tool for me. At a Women's Herbal Symposium I created a Soul Card that represented the horror of my abuse. I went with the raw emotions I was feeling at the time, quickly flipping through magazines as the theme jumped out at me. I tore out pages of crying children, unhealthy sad animals and butchered meat. Trembling and crying as I made my first Soul Card, I was the only one not making a card covered in puppies, flowers and happy children, but I realized that I had to do this hard work. As ugly and painful as it was, I owed it to myself, my inner child, and my future happiness.

Various collages have helped me to focus on what I have experienced and what I desire. Intentional collages are tricky, as you have to be specific in what you ask for. This I knew, yet I, too, made an unintentional collage mistake, though my girlfriend told me to be very clear in what I asked for. She had told me of her experience when she had created a collage created to bring into her life a tall, dark, handsome, sweet, loving, kind, adoring, intelligent, and resourceful man. She did indeed meet and marry a wonderful man who fit her request perfectly. The one problem was that she had forgotten to include wealth in any way at all. He was from another country and unable to work in hers. This became a deal breaker and they divorced two years later.

An intentional collage that I created represented where I would love to live. It contained a small yellow cottage with white trim, lots of windows, located next to a creek, and tucked under trees. It had a gravel walkway, was away from paved roads, had lots of walking trails, playground equipment, large BBQ area, all set in a communal setting.

A few years later, we bought that exact dream house, down to the white trim. What I had failed to include was that the community would be loving, kind, filled with integrity, treating all with equality and having our best interests at heart. In this instance, the opposite was true. Eventually we had to leave in order to get away from all the bad energy. I still miss that lovely yellow cabin along the creek, but I learned a very important lesson about myself in that I need to be aware of what kind of community I create around me and how very important it is for me to be surrounded by loving, safe, sane and amiable people. Not only is it good for me, but it makes me feel good. I am learning who I am as well as what I enjoy doing and who I want to share that with.

SOULTHRIVER

CHAPTER TWELVE

Ralph and I celebrated our twenty-fifth wedding anniversary vacationing for two weeks in Belize. We had dreamed about spending our retirement years there but, during our vacation, I suffered from sun poisoning and a severe reaction to the sand fleas. The environment was not compatible with me. Two years later, we purchased our small cabin, the one I had collaged. We had anticipated our house selling quickly so we took out an interest only loan to purchase the cabin and, two weeks later, Ralph retired. Ralph had received a bonus incentive to retire early and with that money we gutted the cabin, replacing the roof, floors and dry wall. Six months later, we moved into the cabin and put our other house on the market. We were in heaven for six months as we enjoyed hours of soaking in the swimming hole located just down the road, as we waited for the house to sell. The house didn't sell and we were now paying two mortgages, had taken money from Ralph's Thrift Savings and we were maxing out our credit cards. We were getting desperate as our money dried up. Then miraculously we had a buyer for the house with a full price offer. We had a ninety-day escrow, and then the unthinkable happened. On the eighty-seventh day of escrow, the market crashed and our buyer no longer qualified for her loan. We became desperate and put both the house and the cabin up for sale.

We both began working part-time while working on improving the houses so they would sell. It took two and a half years to sell the house, then another three years to sell the cabin. We had lost over a half million dollars in property along with our savings and needed to re-evaluate our priorities. We realized that we could no longer live in the part of California we both loved and grew up in and were looking to find the next best solution. So with our remaining money, we paid cash for a modest house up in the mountains, a scenic two hour drive from our past lives.

We joined the local AA and NA community that was healthy and thriving in our new little town. There was no active Al-Anon group so we decided to create one. Life was once again a daily treat. We were debt-free and completely retired. In no time, the things we were accustomed to began to eat into our budget. We lived a one-hour drive from most shopping; gasoline was now inching up to $5 a gallon. Health, auto, home and fire insurance were climbing. We had put on a new roof, replaced the entire plumbing, installed a new electrical panel and painted our new home. It was then that we realized that we were not going to be happy with just waiting out the rest of our lives. We were no longer content living the American dream, or interested in wearing our grey hair and stooped shoulders, living in a "paid for house" as badges of courage. We could afford what we needed but there was no buffer, no extras for fun, travel or emergencies. We did not want to resort to watching the stock market and the effect it had on our remaining Thrift Savings.

In 1976, Ralph and his best friend had traveled to South America, where it stole his heart. For over thirty years, I heard him romanticize about South America and how much he loved the people there. In the past, we had visited Acapulco, Mexico, Baja California and Belize but all those places had intense weather, to the point where I received sun poisoning. Ralph was talking with a friend one day who had also lived in Colombia about the same time Ralph had been there. Ralph told him how much he wanted to live there but that the weather didn't agree with me. Our friend then suggested we try Ecuador, as most of the country enjoys a gentle climate. When Ralph was in South America, he had spent some time in Ecuador and remembered it fondly.

We began planning and, several months later, we visited Ecuador where I, too, fell in love with it. We returned home, spent lots of time and money getting our four cats documented for travel, and then gathered the paperwork necessary to obtain our retirement visas. All of this was stressful, time-consuming yet exciting. Most people thought we were nuts and I am convinced that that is why we kept the house in California. As long as we had our house, we looked like we were being sensible, and that was the feedback we were getting, but the Universe had other plans for us. After living in Ecuador for five months, our renters became very difficult. We soon realized that we did not need this stress in our lives. We put our house on the market and, in three weeks, we had a full-price offer. We returned to the States to liquidate everything. We had wonderful help from our son and friends and we sold everything!!!

The last day that our son was staying with us, he told me that my parents had removed me from their Will. In the past, I had fantasized what I would someday do with that money. Ten years earlier, they had asked Sean to ask me if I wanted to be in their Will. At first I said no, but then quickly changed my mind. I had spent a lot of time and money healing from the damage they had inflicted on me and I felt entitled. In my mind, I had done nothing to not receive my inheritance. At first, I was devastated to be removed. I felt like I was being punished for being a bad daughter, then I realized that this was a blessing. I now had no ties to my family of origin. They no longer could pull on the invisible threads they had woven throughout my physical and spiritual being. I no longer needed to carry their shame, fear or craziness. I was free to return all that which they had dumped onto me. I was now a happy, capable and free adult who was in charge of my own happiness. And I am living that divine freedom and happiness.

After living for one year in the northern part of Ecuador, we discovered a haven in the southern part of the country where we found a small town that was a virtual twin to the town I grew up in. It is small, quaint, quiet, green, mountainous and spiritual. I have found my tribe and my peace. There are amazing people in my community now who help me with my growth and my potential.

One of my healthier coping skills that I developed as a child was dance. When I needed my daily escape, I would go into my bedroom, with or without music, and I would then close my eyes and dance. It was a great way to escape; I became numb and free as I had created a whole other life outside of me and my surroundings.

When I was older, I enjoyed going to clubs to dance. As I danced I would close my eyes, which gave my dance partner the wrong impression. I felt sensual and acted sensual, which they sensed as sexuality. Sensuality is what I was enjoying, the joy of movement, my body being one with the music, feeling alive. Sexuality, in my mind, was what my dance partners wanted to enjoy with me, or inside me. I was trying to recreate the incredible feeling that dance had brought me in an environment that was commonly referred to as the meat market, clubs where people hooked up for new sexual experiences. I never did leave with anyone. I felt that the dance that I needed was not the same as what was happening in those clubs.

A psychic once told me that I was a dancer in a past life. I believe that bringing dance with me to this life helped save me.

I participated in a Southern California Herbal Symposium where I joined a dance therapy session that was amazing and extremely therapeutic for me. The music had a tribal beat that moved my body's spirit to a healing space as I reconnected (with the help of two dance therapists) with that injured part of me. It was a very emotional experience as I rejoined my sensuality. I began to heal the damage and trauma that I had danced deep into the very DNA of my body. Later, I took belly dance lessons that further healed my wounds. Dancing with other students was an incredible way to be able to connect with my body and with other women. This became a huge part of my healing process as our bodies moved in rhythm with each other.

I have begun attending Ecstatic Dance events and had been to several Dance Therapy sessions and Trance Dance. Here in my new country I again found Ecstatic Dance events. The dance was held in a beautiful green valley surrounded by gorgeous green hills and mountains, set in a large grassy field bordered by trees, with a river on one side and a pond in front. The stage was a beautiful large wooden structure open on three sides, with a roof slanting upwards towards the sky. There was no talking during the two hours that we danced. Before we began dancing, we all sat in a circle and stated our intention for ourselves for that evening's dance.

My one word intention to the group was Release. The music was divine and very loud. There were about twenty of us, men and women, young and old. The music started very slowly, helping us to warm up our bodies and loosen up our moods. As the music intensified the deeper I went, letting my body do whatever it wanted to. The music played was African, Middle Eastern, belly dance music, aboriginal music and more. I became one with the music moving like never before. Halfway through the session an incredible rainbow appeared just above the field. We could see both ends; it was vibrant with color and it lasted more than ten minutes. I was enjoying moving with the music as it became more and more intense. A haunting Spanish song came on with the male singer crying about his broken corazon (heart). I did not understand the words he sang but the emotions in his voice resonated with a deep wounded part of me and I broke down. I was bawling and stomping the ground, hitting the air, fighting off demons, pushing away the bad touching I had experienced in my life. I fought for my body to be mine, to feel safe in my own skin and to feel healed. As I felt the aching for my broken heart I screamed, yelled, sobbed, pulled my hair, beat the floor with my fists until I was crumbled to the ground, trembling with sobs. I melted into release as the music slowly changed to a light comforting melody, bringing lightness to my body as I vibrated with joy. It was important for me to have been witnessed by the other dancers and the half-dozen people who were resting on the grass watching the stage. I was neither embarrassed nor ashamed.

I had done a huge chunk of work that night. When we were done and waiting for our ride home, I sat silently in the dark feeling the new sensations in my body. I was surrounded by beauty and hundreds of fire flies that were dancing in the garden. I felt that I had been witnessed by other souls and spirits as they surrounded me. This dance contained a healing that pushed reality into my brain, my skin, and my bones. Dance has now become a way to reclaim myself, replace the hurt with beauty, the dark with light, the sadness with joy. I am being released by releasing the past. I had mourned and grieved my truth in front of strangers, nature and myself. I felt a new layer surrounding my being as a healthy, safe vibrancy enveloped me.

In my limited knowledge of Astrology, I have learned that there are lunar aspects that relate to the placement of the moon during the time of birth. Your life reflects the stages of the moon which changes every seven-to-eight years. I was born during the darkest phase of the moon, which can be a very sad, dark and introspective time which is not particularly favorable for a new child. When I turned thirty, I was once again at the Lunar Cycle that is called the Balsamic Moon or dark moon. It was during this time that I stopped smoking and stopped talking. It was a very dark time in my life but also a very fruitful time of growth for me as I dove down into the heavy work of recovery to recover myself. This was a time to examine my history, to begin my thirty-year venture of healing and struggle to become a thriver.

Now that I am sixty, I am once again back visiting the Balsamic Moon. I am taking this time to look back at the thirty years of work I have endured. I am now on my third passage of the dark moon, a perfect time to fine-tune myself. I am learning to relax, love myself and truly be with myself. This is also what has led me to writing this book. The Balsamic Moon has taken me deep down to the darkest dark where light seems to have all but disappeared. I am experiencing a feeling of going down deep into Mother Earth, feeling the gritty dark feelings, and acknowledging the darkness I have experienced. It is a time to retreat inward by slowing down. It is the opposite of being in the full moon where life is illuminated with a lot of energy to pull from. I have dove in head first in my recovery process by partaking in whatever became available. I am hoping that my journey will inspire other victims to walk their healing path. We survivors have been burnt to the bone and need to flesh out once again.

Writing this book has been very difficult, yet very healing. Many, many, many days I am feeling heavy or depressed as my body aches. I feel overwhelmed. I want to crawl into a black hole to sleep, and sometimes I do. I would write for maybe half an hour to an hour each morning. It has a life of its own. I am now living in a part of the world where many people have come to write their stories. I bought a used computer to begin typing my story. Much to my frustration, the computer was reacting to my energy. It crashed whenever I typed some of my most painful stories, causing me to retype the story up to ten times before the computer accepted it and, when I tried backing up my work, it failed. This was gut-wrenching for me to have to repeatedly retype these painful memories. Having to pour out my heart over and over again was breaking down my spirit. At the same time, it was making the story real, potent and powerful. There is no denying the emotions I was feeling and projecting onto my computer. I am being reminded that what I have to say is important to me and that it may help others. The truth is often ugly, painful and liberating.

Life has truly turned out better than I could ever have imagined. Every day is a blessing, for I am free to choose what I do as well as where I go. I may choose to garden, go for a walk, hike in the mountains, visit neighbors, swim in the river, do yoga, meditate or have lunch in town. I enjoy sitting for hours in the local coffee shop visiting with friends, making pottery, going to

Spanish class, taking Tango lessons, trying a new recipe, playing with our cats or just lying in my hammock while reading a good book.

I am now a thriver that is enjoying living life for my highest good with my soul intact. I am a SoulThriver. I have a deep connection with the Universe. I see synchronicities in everyday life that tell me that I am a part of the deep healing stream of consciousness that flows around me. I am on my path to be a Master in order to help others, along with myself, claim the title of SoulThriver.

Made in the USA
Columbia, SC
28 November 2017